MW00351998

History & Guide

Portsmouth

Mark Bardell

History & Guide

Portsmouth

Mark Bardell

The
History
Press

For Ruth

First published in 2001 by
Tempus Publishing
Reprinted 2003

Reprinted in 2009 by
The History Press
The Mill, Brimscombe Port,
Stroud, Gloucestershire, GL5 2QG
www.thehistorypress.co.uk

Reprinted 2013

© Mark Bardell, 2009

The right of Mark Bardell to be identified as the Author
of this work has been asserted by him in accordance with the
Copyrights, Designs and Patents Act 1988.

All rights reserved. No part of this book may be reprinted
or reproduced or utilised in any form or by any electronic,
mechanical or other means, now known or hereafter invented,
including photocopying and recording, or in any information
storage or retrieval system, without the permission in writing
from the Publishers.

British Library Cataloguing in Publication Data.
A catalogue record for this book is available from the British Library.

ISBN 978 0 7524 2263 3

Typesetting and origination by
Tempus Publishing
Printed and bound in Great Britain by
Marston Book Services Limited, Oxfordshire

CONTENTS

INTRODUCTION & ACKNOWLEDGEMENTS

From the Napoleonic wars and through a century of empire and two world wars, Portsmouth has been a city of pivotal naval and military importance. Portsmouth and the Navy came to be synonymous. Yet there were always other Portsmouths: a supporting civilian infrastructure, a civilian ferry terminal and port, a seaside resort, a Victorian city and, latterly, a city of education, that grew as the Navy and Dockyard reduced.

Urban boundaries can be traced on a map but Portsmouth's role in the world has taken the city far beyond these. Its real hinterland has always been beyond the horizon – South Georgia, Botany Bay, La Rochelle, Riga, Trincomalee, Minorca, Gibraltar, Nashua, Sebastopol, Vancouver Island, Antigua, Valletta, Halifax, Nova Scotia, Ascension Island, Sullom Voe, Scapa Flow, and so on. It was the port of embarkation for voyages of exploration, transportation and emigration; military expeditions to most wars from the Middle Ages to the twentieth century left from here. Street and pub names record distant places that the fleet sailed to but most citizens knew nothing of at first hand. Portsmouth's local economy was directly war-related and the city's future determined in rooms at the Admiralty and the Foreign Office.

Sailors from HMS Alacrity *– ashore, c. 1900.*

But whose city is it? Most historical narrative chronicles the actions of the rich and powerful; they were the key players in diplomatic and political history and most documentary evidence is about them. The sumptuousness of HMS *Victory*'s Great Cabin is testimony to Nelson's importance as a naval strategist and commander, yet the mess tables and hammocks on board are mute reminders of over 800 others, who mainly survive only as names in a muster book. Yet a city seen through its surviving buildings and artefacts offers up more evidence of history's extras. The built environment is more eloquent of typical lives – the construction worker, dockie, machinist, shipwright, visitor. It is through the medium of this environment that I want to illustrate some aspects of this city's history.

All historical accounts are selective and this selection is the product of a personal viewpoint. It has been assembled from both original research and the secondary work of others and I recognise my debt, particularly, to the historians whose work has been published in the *Portsmouth Papers* over a thirty-five-year period. The bibliography gives some acknowledgement to them and to other historians whose work I have raided. Thanks go to: Jacques Brichet, captain of the *Bretagne*, for a helpful interview and to Robert Siddall of Brittany Ferries for making it possible; the architect Headley Greentree, designer of the Tipner Tri-sail and masts; to Alan King and librarians at the City Library Service who do an excellent job, one that is too infrequently acknowledged, to John Stedman and to Campbell McCutcheon.

Mark Bardell
June 2001

CHAPTER 1

Landfall

When a cross-channel ferry, such as the M/V *Bretagne* out of St Malo, approaches Porstmouth one of the first signs of arrival is the Nab Tower – useful now as a lighthouse but actually a recycled element of a 1918 scheme to install an anti-submarine net across La Manche. Steaming on towards the Southsea shore there are more follies. Sea forts – Spitsand, Horse Sand and Nomansland – were the seaward part of a ring of defensive forts around Portsmouth from a plan inspired by fears of French invasion and devised by Victorian foreign Secretary Lord Palmerston – Britain's first assertive 'firebrand' and later the Crimean War premier.

Past the forts, the ship approaches the Outer Speed Buoy, the start of the Portsmouth Channel, and the Queen's Harbour Master will make contact to grant or deny authorisation to enter the harbour. Waiting for permission is done here. The ship then heads toward the seamark spire of Southsea's St Jude's church, skirting the eastern edge of the navigable water known as Spithead – an area traceable from Gilkicker Point and Southsea Castle to Ryde on Wight's north coast and Nomansland fort. The name derives from the head of the Spit sandbank and with water depth of 12 fathoms and the protective cover of the Isle of Wight it is a fine anchorage and one with historical resonance. Safe anchorage it may be but it has still witnessed the loss of ships: in the eighteenth century the *Resolution* and *Marlborough* (blown up), the *Boyne* (caught fire). In 1782 the *Royal George*, while being careened, was given too much cant and keeled over sinking with the loss of a thousand lives. In 1878 the wooden training frigate *Eurydice* sank suddenly in a squall. Two armed trawlers hit mines and sank in 1940.

This was also the site of a court martial and a mutiny. In 1779 Admiral Augustus Keppel faced a court martial aboard the *Britannia* for dereliction of duty while in action off Ushant. Popular, and also a friend of the king, Keppel was acquitted and had a pub named after him. Twenty-three years earlier the less well-connected Admiral John Byng suffered a different fate. In the spring of 1797 the Channel fleet essentially went on strike over pay grievances. The mutiny lasted a month and its solidarity forced the Admiralty to parley with delegates from the lower deck and agree terms.

Spithead was also the venue for that institution of naval display – the Fleet Review.

The first was in June 1773 when George III came to check out the fleet that was between wars. The Seven Years' War (1756-63) had brought Britain military and naval success, notably at Quebec and Quiberon Bay, but its cost had doubled the national debt. The Exchequer looked to the American colonies as a source of revenue and the resultant taxation without representation helped provoke the American war of Independence in 1775.

In the reign of Victoria these reviews became a popular event with HMS *Warrior* providing the main attraction of the 1867 Review and the Diamond Jubilee Review of 1897 proving the high-watermark of the Imperial Navy. At this, 165 British warships were ordered in rows stretching for five miles towards the open sea. The Royal Yacht *Victoria and Albert*, leading the reviewing flotilla, sailed up and down the columns as the shipboard bands played *God Save the Queen*.

But back to the journey: from the Outer Speed Buoy the ship decreases speed from 16 knots to around 10 knots by Speed Refuge Buoy and lines up to negotiate the deep-water channel close inshore. The approach to the harbour entrance is relatively easy, with enough water everywhere, unlike at St Malo. The channel has been dredged to a depth of 10 metres – enough for aircraft carriers and certainly enough for ferries like *Bretagne* with a draught of 6 metres. The ship's progress parallel to the shore allows passengers a clear view of Southsea Castle. Built as part of a projected defensive chain of castles stretching from Hull to Falmouth, with its angled bastions it was the state of fortification art in 1544. Henry VIII used it as a viewing platform to watch a galley and galleon skirmish with the French in July 1545 and witness the sinking of the *Mary Rose*. The castle was an easy prize for the Parliamentarians in the Civil War.

Still hugging the shore, our vessel passes an esplanade of monuments and memorials, the most visible being the obelisk that is the Royal Naval War Memorial. Further along the shore hovercraft can be seen beached on the slipway. British engineer Sir Christopher Cockerell realised the first workable design in 1950 and a commercial hovercraft was in operation by 1968. This is the perfect vehicle for the Solent crossing to Ryde, currently achieved in just under ten minutes.

Beyond the hover terminal is the modern survivor of Clarence Pier. The original complex dates from the 1860s and was part landing stage and part leisure dome for Victorian visitors. Steam packets linked Portsmouth with other south coast resorts including the Isle of Wight. The Assembly Rooms, destroyed in 1941, gave way to Billy Mannings' Funfair. The Ferris Wheel of the fête foraine signals the start of Old

Clarence Esplanade in the early 1900s.

Clarence Parade, Southsea

The Point seen from a cross-channel ferry approaching the harbour entrance.

Portsmouth's fortifications. This approach to the harbour entrance, flanked by fortifications, was a favourite subject for nineteenth-century seascape painters, including J.M.W. Turner and J. Callow. The stonescape of defensive works was started in the 1680s to the designs of a Dutch military engineer Sir Bernard de Gomme – from Kings Bastion to the Long Curtain, the Square Tower (a former magazine), the 18-gun battery, pierced by the Sallyport gate, to the Round Tower (the city's original fortification, begun in 1418).

Hard by the Tower is the former house of marine artist W.L. Wyllie (1851–1931) with its own tower and spire; which gave Wyllie a view of

the Solent over the Round Tower, a view he used in many of his paintings. The white weather-boarded house jutting out into the fairway is Quebec House – originally a salt-water bathing house, built in 1754. Emigrants for North America departed from the quay. Alongside is the former customs house – the excise men were busy along this coast. This land spit is Portsmouth Point, of cartoon and symphonic fame, and also Spice Island, of run-ashore legend. It is fitting that the Point's prow should be dominated by the Still and West public house and the Spice Island Inn (formerly, in part, the Lone Yachtsman, named following the homecoming on 4 July 1968 of Sir Alec Rose after his single-handed circumnavigation of the globe).

The ripple of a tide race is a reminder of the narrowness of the harbour mouth. The span of the entrance channel from Fort Blockhouse on the Gosport side to Point's Round Tower is 250 yards. Tudor citizens drew comfort from the 'mightie chayne of yron' that stretched from shore to shore as a defensive barrier to the haven's entrance.

Once through the mouth, the harbour opens out and stretches north toward Portsdown Hill. Short of access to the bridge and its panoramic viewing platform 25 metres above the water line, an interested spectator would need to take up the best position forward to survey the unfolding harbourscape both to port and starboard. On the Portsmouth side, behind The Point is revealed the entrance to the Camber – the town's original dock. Soon the new build housing and retail sheds of Gunwharf Quays announce the latest make-over of redundant defence estates. This was the original ordnance yard and wharf, later HMS *Vernon*, the diving and torpedo training schools. Restricted access space has become public space.

Part of the former granary of the Royal Clarence Victualling Yard, Weevil Lane, Gosport, built in 1853 (architect John Rennie the Younger).

The view to starboard from an incoming ferry: HMS Warrior *and the Semaphore Tower (left).*

Looking astern on the port side is the peninsular shore establishment HMS *Dolphin* at the mouth of Haslar Lake. The 100 ft water-tower used for submarine-escape training signals Dolphin's role as a naval submarine base. There have been twenty-two ships of that name in the Navy – one, a sixth rate, took part in two circumnavigations of the globe in the 1760s. In the distance, beyond the marina's thicket of masts, is the water-tower of Haslar Hospital, built between 1746 and 1762, which was then Europe's largest brick building and provided medical care for the Georgian navy.

The sixteen-storey tower blocks with their distinctive gable end mosaics were built in 1964, providing social housing with some of the best views in the country. The flats loom over Ferry Gardens, the entry point to Gosport for waterborne passengers arriving at the town's ferry pontoon. Steam ferries started operating from here in 1869 as an alternative to the floating bridge which was hauled across the harbour between this shore and The Point. The ferry-bridge was made by

The view to port: the Royal Clarence Victualling Yard and jetty.

Acraman of Bristol and towed round to Portsmouth to start operating in May 1840. The viability of the steam launch service was given a boost when Portsmouth Harbour Station was completed in 1876. Easy connections could be made with the London line and the city via the new pier and public landing stage that was a stipulated part of the scheme. The only drawback was that the Portsmouth landing point was by the Hard. This waterfront street by the Dockyard main gate had by then acquired a reputation for brawling and licentiousness and was known as 'Devil's Acre'.

The ferries used in the early 1960s were built at the Gosport yard of Camper and Nicholson – shipbuilders famous for the design and construction of sailing yachts, particularly the *Endeavour* launched in 1934 and designed as an America's Cup challenger. The current Woolston-made ferries still weave across to a landing stage beneath the iron bulk of Portsmouth Harbour station, cantilevered out over the harbour mud. Yachts and small craft must keep to their allocated channel away from the course of the incoming ferry; any boats that stray into the ship's path are warned by several *coups de sirène*.

The black hull of the restored HMS *Warrior* – the Navy's first ironclad warship (1861) – marks the southern frontier of the Dockyard township. The building north of the ship is the Semaphore Tower – part of a dedicated line of communication that connected the naval base with the Admiralty in London. One of the original Portsea town gates (1778) was built into the seaward facade of this 1929 building; naval personnel disembarking at the South Railway Jetty enter the naval base and the city through this gate. From the Tower the Harbour Master controlled all shipping movements across the harbour, including wherries and barges, shallow draught vessels to ferry people and animals, cutters, catamarans, paddle-steamers, smacks, dredgers, steam launches, hoys, schooners, tugs and tenders.

On the Gosport side the Royal Clarence Yard is fronted by a long jetty arcing out into the area known as Weevil Lake. Weevils are insect pests that infest stored grain but also often found their way into ship's biscuit and this signifies Clarence Yard's former role as the local centre for the navy's victualling operations. Burrow Island, by the marina, was once known as 'Rat Island' as ships would dump offal there and open the gun ports to encourage rats to jump ship! From the starboard side there is a clear view of Nelson's flagship, HMS *Victory*, berthed in dry dock since 1922 and before that a familiar sight afloat in the harbour.

As the ferry turns to starboard and approaches the ferry port, there is a collection of buildings at the mouth of Gosport's Forton Creek, fronting a small harbour protected by a mole. This is Priddy's Hard. The oldest building, the gunpowder magazine, was completed in 1777

Main gate of the Royal Clarence Yard, built in 1828.

and was the Navy's Board of Ordnance gunpowder depot. Portsmouth citizens had successfully petitioned George III to have the previous magazine at the Square Tower moved from their midst.

In the upper reaches of the harbour and on Fareham Lake there was storage of a different kind. During the late eighteenth and early nineteenth centuries prison hulks housed both local convicts and prisoners of war. Prisoners often worked on building projects in the area and many were awaiting transportation to Australia. In 1786 a group of prisoners staged a protest about their appalling conditions, which was met with musket fire killing eight prisoners and severely wounding thirty-six. The hulks provided a trade for watermen who ferried the curious out to view the prisoners.

Across from Priddy's Hard our ferry will steer to starboard at North Corner to cross by the tidal basin. From here there is a good view of Portchester Castle across the northern reaches of the harbour. At Fountain Lake Corner as the ship turns to approach its berth at Mile End Quay, it's possible to take in the extent of the Dockyard. It covers almost 300 acres and at its height included a manufacturing rope-house, many storehouses, block mills, a foundry, smithy, bakehouses, brewery, fire station, naval academy, residential terraces and a church. The buildings remain, but many have been recycled with new uses.

At the Continental Ferry Port the ferry docks, bows first. If there's a wind speed of more than 30 knots, a tug waiting at Fountain Lake assists. North west of the the terminal is Whale Island, attached by bridge to the mainland. This convict-built isle was constructed on mud and spoil transported here from Dockyard excavation projects over a thirty-year period. It is designated HMS *Excellent* and was originally the gunnery training school but is now a general training centre.

A moored hulk in Liverpool Docks of the type that became a familiar sight in Portsmouth Harbour in the nineteenth century.

CHAPTER 2

Harbour

History is also about topography. Portsmouth Harbour's great natural haven encompassing 15 square miles of water including lakes and creeks has proved more useful over time than other ports, which silted up and became redundant. It is one of a trio of almost land-locked harbours, with Langstone and Chichester harbours to the east and a sequence of tidal channels, Fareham Creek, the Hamble Estuary and Titchfield Haven, to the west. The shingle beaches around Portsea Island are evidence of a barrier formation that developed over 4,000 years. Lagoons formed behind these shingle barriers account for features such as the Great Morrass in Southsea of which the Canoe Lake is the only remnant of this old open water environment. This is an area without building stone but with clays in abundance, so brick-making has been a regional industry since Roman times.

The local landscape has been changed from time to time. Hence Whale Island was created from the spoil of the 1845 dockyard excavation and so named because the two original islands from which it was made apparently resembled the backs of whales surfacing. Quantities of chalk went to form the polder in the north east harbour on which the IBM campus and motorway interchanges sit. The neighbouring marina village of Port Solent on the upper reaches of the harbour is prime real estate built on rubbish. This development's condominiums look across to the original and focal site of the whole enterprise – Portchester Castle.

Evidence of Acheulean industries (200,000-125,000 BC) in the form of a flint-working site was found at Red Barns, Portchester, while Mesolithic (c. 12,000 BC) sites tend to be further inland, such as at Butser Hill. Discoveries at Fort Wallington and the islands off Farlington Marshes include axes, cores and picks. Excavation work for the M27 turned up three Early Bronze Age urns at Portsdown. Bronze Age artefacts have been found on Portsea Island, dug up during building work for St Mary's Hospital. It's possible that the Iron Age hill forts excavated at Old Winchester Hill and Danebury Ring were part of a chain of forts strung out along the Hampshire and West Sussex chalk downs with the nearest one to Portsmouth located at Butser.

The arrival of the Romans in AD 43 brought the area's time in unlettered prehistory to an end. The invading Augusta legion used a site near Chichester (later Fishbourne Palace) as a supply base and it's

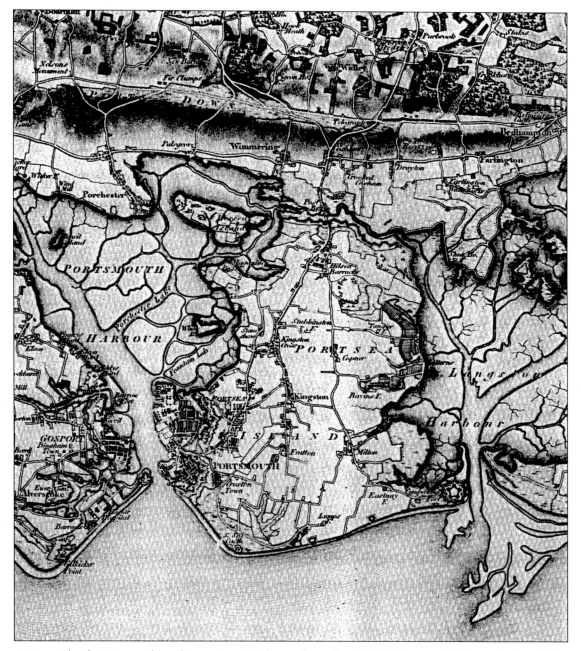

Portsea Island, Portsmouth and Langstone Harbours from the 1811 OS map. (With permission of the Ordnance Survey, NC/01/469)

probable that a small settlement developed around the harbour at Bitterne near Southampton and that a road linked this place and Chichester.

To protect the coast against raids from the sea the Romans appointed a Belgian sailor, Carausius, as commander of the Channel fleet in AD 283. His brief was to eliminate the pirate threat to Belgica and Armorica but Carausius went beyond this and declared himself Emperor of Britain. Rome eventually re-established control in AD 293 when Carausius was assassinated. While in power he initiated the construction of a series of 'Saxon shore' forts that stretched from Portsmouth Harbour to the Wash. It seems probable that the fort at Portchester was one of the first of these. Flint and mortar defensive walls, 10ft thick and 20ft high, enclosed 9 acres and had projecting bastions that could be used as platforms for heavy catapult artillery. This fort appears to have been the garrison for what Barry Cunliffe has called a 'marine commando unit' – a reaction force of galley ships designed to meet a raiding threat.

Following the Norman invasion new building work took place at Portchester Castle creating an inner bailey and keep. The Normans were an army of occupation and needed strongholds for local domination and Britain was to become a French Norman colony with an imported politics and culture. The *Domesday Book* of 1086 records for the Portsdown Hundred churches at Fareham and Bedhampton and includes an entry for Copnor, where human resources were five villeins, two bordars and two serfs and a noteworthy asset was a saltern worth 8d. Wymering, with sixteen villeins, six bordars and two serfs, boasted wood for five hogs.

The Conquest pulled the country's political focus southwards and Portsmouth harbour became an important transit point for royal traffic between the two kingdoms. By 1181 the castle was sufficient for the needs

Portchester Castle, looking toward the moated bailey and the Landgate beyond.

of a resident constable and twenty knights, occasional royalty, a storehouse for royal bullion and for holding significant prisoners. A foundation of Austin canons (following the teachings of St Augustine) built their church within the castle's outer bailey around 1128. Twenty years later this religious house was moved to lands at Southwick where a Priory was established which survived until the Dissolution in the 1530s.

The harbour retained its importance as an arrival and assembly point for fleets and a small settlement formed by the harbour entrance and was formally founded as a town in 1180 by the Norman landowner and entrepreneur, Jean de Gisors. A decade before, he had bought the manor of Buckland, centred on Portsea's highest ground, close to St Mary's church. This manor called Sudewede (Saxon for south water, south wade or causeway) took in the area now known as Old Portsmouth and it was here that Jean de Gisors granted a site to Southwick Priory to build a chapel in honour of Thomas à Becket of Canterbury, Henry II's 'turbulent priest'. The original chancel and transcept are incorporated into the present-day cathedral and the surrounding grid of streets represents the layout of the medieval new town.

Jean de Gisors didn't enjoy his role as town-maker for long as he had to forfeit his lands to Richard I in 1194 as punishment for supporting his usurper brother, John. The Plantagenet king, dubbed the 'Lionheart', ruled from from 1189 until 1199, but he could equally have been called the 'Absent', as he spent a total of six months in the country during his ten-year reign. The Angevin Empire comprised virtually all the western half of modern France as well as England but after only two visits to 'Portesmue', he recognised the town's strategic usefulness as the English gateway to Rouen and Caen. He also needed money for military expeditions and so granted the town its first charter in 1194. The charter conferred the right to hold weekly markets and a fifteen-day annual Free Mart Fair, allowed the town to be exempt from tolls, gave the town's burgesses criminal jurisdiction and made it independent from the county of Southampton. Borough status also put the town under royal control and the modern Portsmouth seal with star and crescent moon date from this time.

The town of Portsmouth grew slowly but in the early 1200s a Domus Dei, or God's House, was established to receive pilgrims and strangers and to be a hospital for eleven local people (it was subsequently the garrison church). Richard's successor John (ruled 1199-1216) lost control of Normandy, Anjou and most of Poitou and was forced to spend more time in England. This brought benefits to Portsmouth one of which was John's decree in 1212 that the royal dock should be 'enclosed with a good and strong wall'. Yet the small town did not prosper and because of its poor defences was vulnerable to raids from across the Channel in times

Cathedral Church of St Thomas, looking towards the organ loft.

Royal Garrison Church, built originally in the sixteenth century as a hospice for pilgrims.

of war. From 1337 for the next hundred years, Portsmouth Harbour was the prime assembly point for outward-bound expeditionary fleets but the town was subjected to French retaliation and was raided and burned in 1338, 1369 and 1380. Pestilence in the form of the Black Death also brought disaster to the young town in 1348-49.

Recognition that Portsmouth needed both military defences and some military control resulted in the start of the construction of earthworks and a moat to enclose the town in 1386 and the appointment of a military governor in 1369. The defensive works were upgraded to stone fortifications with the Round Tower, completed in 1422, and the Square Tower in 1494. An event in 1450 illustrated the potential danger of using the town as an assembly point for expeditionary forces. A force of several thousand had been assembled at Portsmouth but the government delayed the departure of the planned expedition. The redundant combatants were alienated and unpaid. Adam Moleyns, Bishop of Chichester and member of the King's council, made the mistake of visiting the town and as recounted by contemporary chroniclers, Moleyns was taken from the Domus Dei by 'nautis et soldariis' and '..it happid that with boiste[rou]s langage...they fil on him, and cruelli there kilde him.' His death may have been a political assassination but the town was punished by a decree of Greater Excommunication, depriving it of organised religion for the next fifty-eight years. Unhappy militias were to be a source of continuing problems as would the clashes between military and civil jurisdictions.

Portchester Castle's importance as a military site declined during the fourteenth century but with the coming of the Tudors in 1485, Portsmouth's importance rose. In 1495 Henry VII ordered the construction of the country's first graving dock at Portsmouth; this dry dock was completed in eleven weeks and was the forerunner of the industrialising dockyard of the eighteenth century. Two years later, work started on the first warship to be built at the Portsmouth yard – the *Sweepstake*.

Henry Tudor's successor, Henry VIII, was even more concerned with nautical affairs. He took a personal interest in the design of ships and was prepared to spend money on their construction; some of these funds came from the Dissolution of the Monasteries. The king's antagonistic foreign policy towards the French and his success in uniting Europe's two Catholic superpowers against him after breaking with Rome – led to the need to improve Portsmouth's state readiness for war. In 1538 Henry decreed a programme of castle-building as coastal defence – an update of the Saxon shore forts – in this case stretching from Hull in Yorkshire to Falmouth in Cornwall. In the Solent area Hurst Castle staked out the Needles passage, Calshot Castle oversaw Southampton Water and Southsea Castle (built in six months in 1544) guarded the approach to Portsmouth Harbour. Situated on the southernmost tip of Portsea Island, it overlooked the stretch of Solent used by approaching ships negotiating the deep water channel close to the shore. The basic Tudor design placed

The Square Tower was completed in around 1494. It was used from the late sixteenth century as a powder magazine and from the late 1770s as a naval meat store. In 1823 a semaphore station was added to the top.

Southsea Castle looking to the west.

a square stone keep in a surrounding bailey yard and located elevated gun platforms on the outer curtain wall. A dry moat completed the defence. Straight lines converged to form sharply angled bastions – it was cutting-edge fortress design. As we have seen the castle acted as a grandstand in 1545 for Henry to watch his ships take on a French fleet of more than 200 carracks and galleys in the Solent. The king had commissioned ships to be built at Portsmouth Dockyard and some of these were in the English fleet that July day. One of them, the *Mary Rose* – named after Henry's catholic zealot daughter Mary Tudor – had been rebuilt there in 1536 to give her a complete lower deck of guns. She was the pride of the English fleet. Stacked with over ninety iron and cast-bronze guns, her decks and the castles at the stern and bow were crowded with gunners, mariners, archers, soldiers and trumpeters. The engagement proved to be more stand-off than set to. But disaster struck as the *Mary Rose* heeled dangerously and was swamped through her lower deck gunports. She sank almost immediately with an estimated loss of almost 700 men. Over-manning and an unruly crew seem to have accounted for it. Some salvage was attempted at the time but the ship lay, largely preserved in silt, beneath the Solent until its dramatic salvage and recovery in 1982.

Portsmouth itself was already in decline in 1545 and this was to continue throughout the reign of Elizabeth I (1558-1603) as the port became of secondary strategic importance. Maritime rebuilding continued but mostly at the yards nearer to London, Deptford, Woolwich and Chatham, as these were better placed to meet the main threat from

Spain and its base in the Low Countries. The town was struck by plague in 1563 and in 1557 and 1576 extensive fires destroyed royal storehouses near the Camber. Fire of a different kind arrived in 1585 when Francis Drake brought back the would-be settlers from Ralegh's first attempt to establish a colony in Virginia and some of the returning migrants consoled themselves with the aid of tobacco leaves and pipe-smoking was introduced into England.

The North American connection continued into the seventeenth century with the maritime and entrepreneurial activities of Captain John Mason (?1586-?1635). He had been governor of Newfoundland for six years from 1615 where he managed the fishing industry, mapped the island and made expeditions from there to map the territories later known as Nova Scotia, Maine and New Hampshire. He returned to England to live in Portsmouth in 1621 looking for capital and land grants to carry forward his colonising projects. He found employment as Surveyor of Ships for the Navy and enjoyed the patronage of Charles Villiers, Duke of Buckingham, Lord High Admiral, military adventurer and favourite of both James I and Charles I. Mason secured patents on land between the Merrimac and Piscataqua rivers – to be the territory of New Hampshire – and pursued various schemes to make it a settled reality. It was not achieved in Mason's lifetime but he left his family the American lands in his will. The native Susquehanna, we may assume, were not party to the discussions!

In the 1620s England was at war with France and Spain and John Mason's naval post involved him in the military adventures launched by Charles Villiers. These expeditions against Cadiz and La Rochelle (1627) were ill-disciplined failures and costly in lives. The Duke of Buckingham was back in Portsmouth the following year, planning another expedition

Portsmouth (USA) on the banks of the Piscataqua River was New Hampshire's colonial capital until the Revolutionary War. It is also an important nineteenth-century Navy Yard and regional beer-making centre.

This small High Street house with a grand eighteenth-century front was the site of the murder of the Duke of Buckingham in August 1628.

to La Rochelle and stayed at John Mason's house, the Greyhound in the High Street, when fate caught up with him. Not for the first time the town was filled with an expeditionary force which was tense and restless. John Felton, a survivor of the first La Rochelle expedition and harbouring a grievance over a promotion issue, arrived on the morning of 28 August 1628 intending to kill Buckingham. The details of what happened are not clear but on finishing breakfast on that day the duke walked into the hall, amid a throng of people, and Felton reached over someone else to stab Buckingham in the upper chest. The victim died almost immediately. The assailant sat for a while in the kitchen amid the tumult and then gave himself up. The Duke of Buckingham had been due to meet the King that day in Southwick, so news of his murder did not have far to travel. The king was distraught, the populace less so. John Felton asserted that through his deed 'he should do his country a great good service' but he was hanged at Tyburn and then hung in chains on the common at Portsmouth. A memorial to the Duke of Buckingham was erected in the cathedral church of St Thomas.

Within twenty years of coming to the throne (1625), Charles had provoked the Scots, the Puritans, Parliament and whole sections of the population into opposition. His early fondness for costly military adventures hadn't helped, nor had his reliance on the incompetent and unpopular Duke of Buckingham. Ship Money, a levy on port towns to finance the navy, had been extended inland and was deeply resented. Inspite of a programme of naval improvements, most of the navy sided with the Parliamentarians, who were aware of the navy's and Portsmouth's strategic importance in preventing military help reaching Charles from abroad. The town's governor Colonel George Goring had declared for the King in the month before the start of the conflict in 1642. In August the Parliamentarians under William Waller assembled an assault force in the areas behind Portsmouth, seized Portsbridge and laid siege to the town. But this 'siege' was to be a short-lived affair. Platforms for ordnance were set up on the Gosport shore with the guns targeted at the cathedral tower, the town's highest point; one shot was sent through the tower, which did 'brake one of the bells.' Parliamentary troops were ferried over to the Isle of Wight and they captured key forts and Carisbrooke Castle (later a prison for Charles I). Yet the decisive action was to be the capture of Southsea Castle. On the night of 3 September a Parliamentary force, estimated at 400 infantry and 80 musketeers, made their way from Portsbridge, down past Portsea farms and across the common between the two morasses to the castle. After a confused attempt to parley, they stormed the castle and took it. Inside was a complement of twelve with a drunken commander. This was the final blow to a town where morale was low and the number of desertions high. So a deal was struck between Governor Goring and General Waller. The terms were generous to the Royalists, in recognition of their threat to blow up the town's gunpowder magazines. Deserters apart, Royalist gentlemen and their followers were allowed to go and Goring went into exile in Holland. Portsmouth was ceded to the Parliamentarians.

CHAPTER 3

Dockyard

The Parliamentarians beat the English Royalist forces in the First Civil War (1642-46) and then its New Model Army had to do the same to the combined English and Scots Royalists in the Second (spring/summer 1648). King Charles' continuing intransigence and his presence as a focus for anti-Parliamentary sentiment led to his trial and execution in 1649. The period of the Commonwealth, Republic or Interregnum, depending on your politics, up to 1660 was a time of intense naval activity and the start of development for Portsmouth Dockyard. The trade war with the Dutch from 1652 confirmed the Thames estuary as the ship-building and naval centre but Portsmouth was still a useful operational base from which to launch sallies against foreign privateers and to protect East India merchantmen. The three Commissioners at the State's Yard at Portsmouth during that time, William Willoughby, Robert Moulton and Francis Willoughby, were conscientious and purposeful. The latter initiated work that was the basis of Dockyard development over the next 150 years; he carried out a survey of the Yard and oversaw the building of a tar house, rope yard and two rope walks and a dry dock.

Portsmouth was well-placed for the maintenance and refitting of ships patrolling the Channel; it was hard by the 'commodious anchorages' of St Helens, Stokes Bay and Spithead; ordnance supplies of shot and cannon could be brought from the Wealden iron industries and powder from the mills at Guildford. Victuals could not be provided from local supplies alone and meat, for instance, was brought by ship from the salting house and cooperage at Tower Wharf. In 1650 a ship was built at the yard, the first since 1509, and then a frigate in the form of the 50-gun *Laurel* whose construction was overseen by the master shipwright then, the aptly named Mr Boate. This shipbuilding, which continued for subsequent decades and the yard's re-fitting function made Portsmouth into an entrepot, importing material from all points: tar, tallow, turtle-irons, oak treenails, hemp, hearths, duck; canvas from Bridport and Brittany, iron from the Forest of Dean, masts from Sweden and New England, cordage from Russia. Where more local sources were available, they were used. So Mr Boate and officers surveyed for timber within six miles of Portsmouth; and the reconnaissance of trees continued through Sussex, the New Forest, the Isle of Wight, Salisbury, Woodstock, the Forest of Bere. This enterprise was neither Republican nor Royalist and Dockyard operations were expanded after the Restoration. When the Commonwealth looked as if it would descend into a junta of generals, troops from different parts, including a contingent from Portsmouth, marched on London to restore Parliament. By early 1660 it had voted to return to the monarchy and Charles Stuart was invited back to become Charles II. Some statesmen managed to make the transition to the new regime and one of them was Edward Montagu, who had been a general-at-sea in the Commonwealth and kept some residual monarchist sympathies in reserve. At the Restoration he was made Earl of Sandwich and as he rose he determined that his secretary and cousin should similarly prosper. So Samuel Pepys also rose.

Samuel Pepys (1633-1703), although a life-long Londoner, was to be a significant figure for Portsmouth because he made naval administration ship-shape and modern. From his initial installation as Clerk of the Acts to the Navy Board in 1660 until his promotional peak as First Secretary to the Admiralty in 1678, he was the main mover in transforming the Navy into a powerful ordered fighting force and the Lord High Admiral's office into an efficient government department. He set out an establishment with grades of employment defining duties, pay discipline and conditions of service. Pepys was a Restoration Man: a Latin classics scholar, informed in mathematics and shorthand, frequenter of tavern and playhouse, skilled diarist, bibliophile, collector of female companions, musical composer and enthusiastic player of the flute, viol and flageolet; 'music and women I cannot but give way to, whatever my business is.' By his drive and hard work Pepys managed to keep a creaking and under-funded navy supply system going during the Second Dutch War (1665-67). The stress he suffered in his post possibly led to severe eye strain and a belief he was going blind; as a precaution he gave up writing his diary in 1669. This document, begun in 1660 and written in shorthand, is one of the great personal records of contemporary life. Pepys was an occasional visitor to Portsmouth: in 1662 to await the arrival from Lisbon of Catherine of Braganza, Charles II's bride; in 1683 to embark on an expedition to wind up operations in the failing base of Tangier, a port that had been part of Catherine's dowry, and to make tours of inspection of the Dockyard. He wanted to know everything about the world he was responsible for; he got a clerk to teach him sailors' jargon and he familiarized himself with production line procedures – I 'walked in the rope yard, where I do look into the tar houses and other places and took great notice of all the several works belonging to the making of a cable.' Yet he confided to his journal that he could play the committee dissembler; he wrote about a meeting to decide on a building contract for the construction of a Mole, where seemingly none of the committee understood the terms demanded but agreed anyway... 'and so I left them to go on to agree, for I understood it not.' In 1685 Pepys became an MP and master of Trinity House, a seventeenth-century guild set up to promote and protect shipping around England's shores and later responsible for seamarks, the training of pilots and building and maintenance of lighthouses. He had intended to write the definitive account of the history of the Navy but had to be content with an interim *Memoires relating to the State of the Royal Navy*. As it was he created a great storehouse of research materials by leaving his papers and library of 3,000 books on his death in 1703 to his *alma mater*, Magdalene College, Cambridge.

The operating Navy that Pepys bequeathed came to be increasingly relied on as the eighteenth century wore on. Continental rivalries were stretched, geographically, from the New World to the Indian Ocean, and maritime efficiency and power would arbitrate in disputes over colonies and trade. Wars with the Dutch shifted the focus of operations to the Thames and the East coast; wars with the French put Portsmouth back in the frame.

France and England fought during the 1740s and again in 1754 in North America; skirmishes that were eventually became formalised as the Seven Years War (1756-63). An early naval rebuff resulted in a court martial. In 1756 Admiral John Byng had been sent with an understrength squadron of ships-of-the-line to relieve the besieged island of Minorca. After an indecisive encounter with the French, Byng withdrew to regroup

Old Portsmouth. A rare surviving street that includes three seventeenth-century Dutch-gabled town houses: Nos 1, 2, and 3 Lombard Street.

at Gibraltar. The island fell to the French and Byng was relieved of his command and brought back to England to face a court martial. Convicted of having failed to do his utmost to save the island, Byng was sentenced to death; and on 14 March 1757 he was shot by a firing squad on the quarterdeck of HMS *Monarch* in Portsmouth Harbour. Defeatist or realist, Byng was a scapegoat; his fate led the French satirist Voltaire to observe that in England they shoot the occasional Admiral 'pour encourager les autres'.

St George's church, St George's Square, Portsea, built 1754.

The Island of Portsea still only had town colonies in its south west corner for much of the eighteenth century. Its edge was defined by mudflats with salterns at the Copnor shore and the interior was mostly farmland, interspersed with common land and marsh. Desmaretz's map of 1750 shows the town of Portsmouth as a fortress with bastions jutting aggressively into the landscape. This was the legacy of the Dutch military engineer Bernard de Gomme during the Restoration, and his complex of bastions, outworks and water barriers had been extended to Gosport, the Dockyard and Portsea. The pesthouse for plague sufferers, built just before the Great Plague of 1665, and sited close by the present-day Mile End roundabout, was still suitably distant from population centres in 1716.

Portsmouth was penned in by fortifications and so Portsea became the boom town. A guidebook of 1775 describes its transformation, 'from a barren desolate heath it is now become a very populous genteel town, exceeding Portsmouth itself in the number of its inhabitants and edifices.' One was St George's church built as a local alternative to the distant St Mary's. St George's Square and Lion Terrace were fashionable addresses and Queen Street (named after Queen Anne) a fashionable shopping street. The 1801 census records Portsmouth's population as 7,839 and that of Portsea as 24,327.

Pub gable-end mural of Thomas Rowlandson's cartoon – 'Portsmouth Point 1800'.

Still the old town could boast run ashore haunts, suitably isolated across the Camber on the Point. Thomas Rowlandson's cartoon - Portsmouth Point - portrays the lewd revelry of legend - a Georgian Skagway. Investigation by the Borough Constables in 1716 revealed forty-one public houses, brandy shops and coffee shops, crammed on to this small spit of land.

The Royal Naval Academy (later College) was founded in 1729 and with a modest intake of forty students, aged 13-16, aimed to teach, over three years, seamanship, navigation, mathematics, astronomy, gunnery, physics and fortification. This was not the usual training for officers but it demonstrated a more professional intent by the Navy. The Desmaretz map shows the Great Ship Basin, completed in 1698 to a design by Edward Dummer, Surveyor to the Navy Board. This non-tidal basin and dry dock was innovatory in conception and scale. His scheme marked the beginning of a programme of planned improvements that, especially after 1760, accelerated to ensure that Portsmouth was the country's premier Yard by the end of the century.

The 1775 guidebook talks of the Dockyard as resembling 'a town in the number of its dwelling houses, offices, storehouses, lofts and other edifices'. The Dockyard was in the process of becoming its own company town – a walled-off enclave – that by the scope and concentration of its craft-based industry, anticipated the industrial town sites of the nineteenth century. There was familiar architecture, such as the Queen Anne terrace (Long Row, 1717) to house principal officers; the Georgian Naval Academy with lantern tower and cupola and the original St Ann's chapel, paid for by naval subscription and dockers' subsidies. Less familiar in their scale and function were the 310-foot long Rigging Store, the three-quarters of a mile-long Great Ropehouse (1770) where eighty men could toil, making one cable or the trio of storehouses (1763-1782), Nos 11, 10 and 9 (Present Use, Middle and South Stores). These were functional sheds with English bond redbrick facades, given rhythm by stone-dressed and keystone-arched windows. Also dry-docks, with stepped sides and wooden treadmill cranes, added to this landscape. The South Office Block was new in 1786 and is arguably the world's first office building.

The Royal Dockyards were the country's largest civilian employer with a workforce of over 15,000 in the home yards by 1814. Employment was uncertain and the peacetime schedule of a 'day and a tide' replaced the wartime full week. Yet the demands of war work did give dockies some leverage and there were Georgian industrial disputes over piecework. The artisan hierarchy was craft-based with Master Boatbuilders or Sailmakers at the top and under them a workforce (according to Navy estimates of 1784) of shipwrights (767), caulkers, oakum boys, smiths, carpenters, sailmakers, riggers, scavelmen, sawyers (134), spinners (117), hatchellers and blockmakers. The latter were made largely redundant by technology when Marc Brunel, father of the more famous Isambard, installed machines for making pulley blocks in the Yard's wood mills after 1802. The new machines allowed ten men to produce 140,000 pulley blocks in a year; previously the work of 110 craftsmen.

The role of the Yard was to build, repair and maintain ships. The Royal Dockyards' slips were used for building the bigger warships, all the three-deckers. Every new ship was fitted out at a yard with a copper bottom and with masts, sail and rigging, most of which was made there. The Yard had to maintain the ships 'in ordinary' (laid up) and maintain the various support craft, such as the hulks used as receiving ships for new recruits and crews of ships under repair, and assorted transports, gigs, wherries, longboats, cutters and launches used for carrying men and supplies. Dockyard security and precautions against fire were perennial concerns. A disastrous yard fire was started by pro-American saboteur Jack the Painter in 1777 but the incidence of embezzlement, corruption and theft was harder to quantify.

In the 1780s, in the upper reaches of the Harbour north from Priddy's Hard, out across the Ouze (the mud banks are so-called on the 1716 map), was moored a squadron of prison hulks. This was 'Campbell's Academy' created by an Act of 1776 and so-named after the first Overseer. On the Statute Book at that time there were 100 offences that attracted the death penalty, some of which were commutable to transportation. The American War of Independence and the closure of the thirteen colonies as places to send deviants had thrown the Georgian penal system into crisis until another 'gulag' was found in Australia and Van Diemen's Land. In May 1787 the First Fleet including convict ships set out from Portsmouth to a virtual blank on the map. The hulks were used as holding prisons for transportees and later, during the Napoleonic wars, to incarcerate prisoners of war. The conditions on the hulks were appalling and prisoners incarcerated on them suffered dysentery, diarrhoea, lung complaints typhus, scurvy and scrofula. They were a 'temporary expedient' but remained in use for almost seventy-five years.

Samuel Johnson (1709-1784), critic and lexicographer, is quoted as saying, 'No man will be a sailor who has contrivance enough to get himself into jail, for being in a ship is being in a jail, with the chance of being drowned'. Certainly the condition of jack tar was nasty, brutish and confined; if he was going to succumb it would mostly be through disease. A first-rate ship of the line, such as HMS *Victory*, with about 100 guns, needed a complement of between 820 and 850 men, mostly to man the guns. Lower deck life was crowded and unhygienic with most of the crew eating at mess tables between the guns and sleeping in hammocks

The quarterdeck of HMS Victory.

slung over the guns; typhus and lice were endemic, it was cramped and there was no privacy. Officers were quartered in stern cabins up-wind from the stench of the ship's company. Navy Board figures for 1776-80 show that while 1,244 men had been killed in action, 18,545 had died from other causes, mostly disease. In theory there was one surgeon to 200 but recruiting good surgeons was hard as many were deterred by the conditions. The vital properties of limes and lemons had been discovered by Captain Cook but their introduction into the seamen's diet was slow. In 1753 the Navy opened a hospital at Haslar on Gosport's southern peninsula. At that time it was the largest brick building in Europe and provided rational medical care, with trucks to bring patients from jetty to hospital on a 'railway' and with an isolation block that had direct access to the Solent. The building testified to the Navy's commitment to health and it confined the sick to one site, bounded by a wall and patrolled by Royal Marines! Absconding was a problem and desertions between 1776 and 1780 were estimated at 42,000.

Defiance was sometimes a group activity. Mutinies at the Nore, Yarmouth and Spithead in 1797 were high profile examples but others are recorded for the early 1780s and throughout the 1790s. Naval service was indeterminate, men could be away for years at a time and even on return, crews could be confined to their ships. When the *Royal George* foundered at Spithead in 1782 it has been estimated that 400 visiting prostitutes were aboard. Recruitment to the Navy was thus problematic and when the numbers supplied by volunteers, foreigners or through the quota system were not enough, impressment was used.

Given the conditions how did the Georgian Navy become such a formidable fighting force? The reasons are complex but include factors such as fear, training and good leadership. Fear of the French was tangible. In the late 1770s it was fear of the capture of Portsmouth and its conversion into a 'French Gibraltar'; in the Napoleonic era the fear was of invasion. The gun crews effectively trained to become synchronised teams. The Navy produced some competent captains and winning admirals: Howe, Rodney, Collingwood, Saumarez, and pre-eminently, Horatio Nelson (1758-1805). The son of a Norfolk rector, he rose to be the country's leading naval tactician and commander, with innate gifts of leadership. He inspired his captains, or 'band of brothers' (his term), into devotion and self-belief . He led from the front and his campaign wounds were badges of this. He left Portsmouth for Cape Trafalgar on 14 September 1805, already the fêted victor of the battles of the Nile and Copenhagen; he was fatally wounded at Trafalgar and his body was returned to Spithead aboard HMS *Victory* on 4 December. He was entombed in St Paul's Cathedral and became a naval icon, memorialised forever in the central square of the Imperial Metropolis.

Semaphore tower at Chatley Heath, Surrey, one of a line of semaphore stations linking the Admiralty to Portsmouth in the early nineteenth century.

In 1796 the Admiralty inaugurated its shutter telegraph link with Portsmouth. Previously a messenger carried an order from Their Lordships by post chaise and rowing boat out to the fleet in the Solent. Without mishap the delivery time was eight hours. The telegraph using a sequence of shutters operated by ropes could send a message from the Admiralty roof via a sequence of hilltop stations to Southsea Common and the Solent in fifteen minutes. The news of the victory at Trafalgar was carried from Falmouth the 270 miles to London by a series of horse-riders in 38 hours. The Plymouth telegraph link was not opened until 1806. Ten years later the shutter was supeceded by the semaphore telegraph which operated along a line of stations from the Admiralty, via Chelsea and Chateley Heath, to Portsmouth's Square Tower.

In July 1775 Captain James Cook arrived back at Portsmouth after the second of his three epic voyages exploring and charting the Pacific and Southern oceans and trying out Harrison's chronometer for measuring longitude. Although ill-fated, Captain William Bligh's expedition had also had a cartographic purpose and, Broadsides apart, even the eighteenth-century Navy was now concerned with shrinking the world and mapping it.

CHAPTER 4

Suburban Resort

In 1853 an anonymous correspondent travelled down to Portsmouth by train to gather material for two articles for a magazine, *The Home Companion*, which were published in August of that year. Rail access to Portsmouth had been established six years before but our correspondent would have travelled either via Eastleigh or Brighton, as the direct route from London was still another six years away. From the moment his train rattled over the drawbridge that breached Hilsea Lines the writer was much taken with the fortified town and the ever-present military; 'the general panoply of war is of such frequent exhibition in Portsmouth.' He booked into a sitting room at the Quebec Hotel – with its view of the floating bridge – and set off on an itinerary that would have impressed any modern tourism officer; first to the Dockyard ('the guides are extremely civil') to view the rope house, the tarring house, block-making machinery; then out to visit HMS *Victory*; later a tour round the Royal Yacht, *Victoria and Albert* ('Her Majesty was most affable and kind to all on board' an officer confided to our correspondent); across to Haslar Hospital and its Museum of Natural History; on to the new bathing station at Anglesey 'contiguous to Alverstoke'; then purchased a ticket for the steam-packet to Ryde.

Back on the mainland he was much taken with Southsea Common, opining that there were few 'more beautiful spots than this plain,' thanks in no small part, he surmised, to the 'schemes of beautification contrived by Lord Frederick Fitzclarence'. Latterly, he reviewed a company of Connaught Rangers on field manoeuvres on the plain. In summation, he concluded that Southsea was 'a sort of compromise between a fortified place and a watering place'. And so it was. A map of the Island of Portsea of 1833 shows the bastion-defined, landward side of the town and outside these walls and southwards marks the Kings Rooms. These were on the site of the later Clarence Pier and comprised assembly rooms for balls and card parties, a pump room, reading room and baths. A contretemps at one of these balls resulted in England's last fatal duel, fought at Browndown. Nearby were beach locations for bathing machines. Stretching towards Southsea Castle, Southsea Common tapers to a narrow strip between the castle and Lumps Fort, hemmed in to the north by the Great Morass. North of that Dock Mill, Marmion Place and the Jews' Burial Ground on Lazy Lane (now Fawcett Road) are all marked as separate sites in open country with farms to the east. The embryonic Southsea is represented by houses along Kings Road and Landport, Hampshire, Kings and Jubilee Terraces (these last two derive from the 1810 Golden Jubilee of George III). Development to the south of Kings Road was named Croxton Town after the landowner and provided housing for artisan families. In contrast the Regency Terraces attracted middle-class migrants from the restriction and constriction of a garrison-controlled town.

The Ordnance Survey map of 1856 shows a solid band of high-density housing stretching up to the railway terminus (now Portsmouth and Southsea station), more sporadic house building tracing the central streets of modern Southsea and the beginnings of development along Albert Road – New Southsea to the north and Nelsonville to its south. This depicts the continuing story of what R.C. Riley has called 'the growth of Southsea as a naval satellite'. The census of 1851 and that of 1861 both record that the heads of almost half the households were serving or retired naval or military officers, with a majority still active naval officers. Civil servants employed by the War Office or Admiralty also lived in suburban Southsea. Along with clergymen, the retired and the property-owning, those in the manufacturing, construction, brewing and clothing trades, lodging house keepers and schoolmistresses were also there. The census returns also reveal another index of Southsea's bourgeois status. Females comprised over 70 per cent of the population in 1851 and 1861. Traditionally the daughters of middle-class families remained at home until they could be married and the running of these households required young women to live in as servants.

The needs of the Army kept the Common clear of speculative developments and provided the green zone that is such a feature of Southsea today. The plain furnished the spectacle of soldiers at drill or playing war games but also pitches for cricket and, further east, opportunities for shooting game. Sea rowing was a possibility and sea bathing was enhanced by a beach that sloped steeply into deep water. Some of this sea water was pumped into the Regency leisure complex of the Kings Rooms to supply showers and vapour baths; and all these amenities were only a stroll away from your villa.

The primary builder of such villas was an architect who remains a hero of Portsmouth's townscape – Thomas Ellis Owen (1804-1862). He was born in Dublin of an architect father, who was Clerk of the Works at Portsmouth in 1820. Thomas was one of seventeen children, five of whom followed their father's profession.

Thomas Owen was a true Victorian entrepreneur. He was adept at surveying and land valuation, design and speculation and Southsea was there for the developing. He contributed to railway and civil engineering projects, including work on the Camber Docks, designed

Netley Terrace, Southsea, built around 1840 and designed by Thomas Ellis Owen.

Sussex Road, Southsea, one of Thomas Owen's picturesque streetscapes from the 1850s.

a church, a chapel and some buildings for the Portsea Island General Cemetery Company. During a first phase, from about 1835 to 1851, he built stuccoed-brick terraces and Italianate villas, mostly to the west of Palmerston Road and around Grove Road. In a second phase, from around 1851 to 1860, Owen built a variety of individual villas, set in picturesque roadscapes, such as in Clarendon Road, the area south of Elm Grove and further east around Florence and Eastern Villas Road. As centrepieces to the emerging suburb, Owen built Portland Place with the Portland Hotel and St Jude's church (1851) as a focal points and a seamark. It has been possible to attribute some seventy-five villas and fifty-four terraced houses to Owen. Given the range of his building and their landscaped settings, especially those around Clarendon and Villiers Roads, it could be claimed that he created the first garden suburb.

Owen was also active in other areas such as local business, politics and social reform. He invested in the Floating Bridge scheme and the local brick-making trade, was twice town mayor and an advocate of sanitation improvements. It is likely that he was also one of the 'movers' behind the artisans' model housing project that resulted in the Friary in Marmion Road. As historian Sarah Quail has said, Owen could be described as '*the maker of modern Southsea*'.

The scramble for development continued apace throughout the mid-1800s. As the residential suburb was developed so the Common and the seafront were improved. Clarence Esplanade was built in the late 1840s creating a permanent pedestrian way linking the Kings Rooms site and Southsea Castle and the railway arrived in Portsmouth in 1847. Its comparatively late arrival was partly due to problems of topography

'Thomas Owen's Southsea', a detail from the 1867 OS 25-inch map. (With permission from the Ordnance Survey, NC 01/469)

but economics and the army had both put their brakes on development. Eventually Portsdown Hill was circumvented, Port Creek bridged and Hilsea Lines breached, despite the resistance of Army strategists. The coming of the railway launched the take-off of Southsea as a resort. By 1870 over 500,000 people a year were using Portsmouth station and the number of lodging houses and hotels available in Southsea was rising rapidly. The Queens Hotel opened in 1861, Beach Mansions in 1866, the Sandringham in 1871 and the Pier Hotel in 1865. The King's Rooms were refurbished in the 1860s and then in the 1870s converted into the Esplanade Hotel. Nearby, Southsea's first proper pier, the Clarence Esplanade Pier was opened in 1861 – essentially as a landing stage for steam packets. By 1865 a tram service connected the pier to the main railway station and the area was starting to become a speculator's dream. By 1872 it was estimated that 200,000 people per year were paying to walk down the pier and in the summer of 1874 gatekeepers were employed to try to sort out the 'riff-raff' from the more genteel pier walkers. This attempt to segregate the classes caused much local resentment that was made worse when the pier company closed a section of road between the pier and the Esplanade Hotel. The new barricades denied public access to Old Portsmouth via the beach and Sallyport and as protesting crowds gathered the barricades were dismantled. Days of assembly, action and reaction culminated in the mayor reading the Riot Act to a crowd of several thousand. Troops and the police were called in to clear the crowd and heads were broken and arrests made. The Pier Company directors relented and the barrier was not replaced. While no Peterloo Massacre, this bit of direct action by Portsmouth and Southsea residents is an important early example of an effective 'people's protest'. The 'Battle of Southsea' lives on in a painting that is now in the City Museum after years hanging in the Barley Mow pub in Castle Road. The demonstration took place at possibly the peak of Clarence Pier's fortunes: from 1876 the new Harbour Station was to siphon off the Isle of Wight traffic and South Parade Pier (opened 1879) was to prove a counter-attraction. Clarence Pier was eventually destroyed in an air raid in 1941.

One day in September 1882 a young doctor stepped off the steamer at Clarence Pier. He had been an apprentice ship's doctor on a whaler

The Queens Hotel,
Southsea.

Lorne Lodge, Campbell Road, Southsea, childhood home of Rudyard Kipling.

York Terrace, Fawcett Road, Southsea, built around 1890.

to the Arctic, spent time as a medical officer on the Liverpool-Sierra Leone steamship run and suffered a failed business venture in Plymouth. He hoped for better things in Southsea where he put up his nameplate at 1 Bush Villas in prosperous Elm Grove. Dr Arthur Conan Doyle (1859-1930) was set to make his fortune but not from medicine. Medical business was slow and between his infrequent consultations he began scribbling stories for publications in magazines such as *Boy's Own Paper*. By 1886 he had finished a novella, *A Study in Scarlet* which, when published in 1887, represented a milestone in modern detective fiction. By linking scientific methods to crime detection in his fiction he was reflecting developments in real policework of the time and the book sold well. Although the author wanted to write historical romances, he wrote *Micah Clarke* and *The White Company* in Southsea, the demands of his public and his publishers ensured that he spent the next forty years turning out Sherlock Holmes stories. Conan Doyle was a sociable, vigorous and sporting character such that when he left Southsea in 1890 he left a record other than his books behind. He was an active member of the Portsmouth Scientific and Literary Society and was familiar with Dr James Watson, its president. He was a player-member of Portsmouth Cricket Club and a founder member of Portsmouth Amateur Football Club for whom he played as goalkeeper.

As Conan Doyle struggled with diagnoses and plots, a couple of hundred yards westwards, in Hyde's Emporium on King Street, another writer to be, the young Herbert George Wells (1866-1946), was struggling with life as a draper's assistant. Wells moved to London and found his escape in education, graduating in zoology from the Normal School of Science in London and began his own writing career startng with biology and geography textbooks but moving later into books on a variety of social issues and, of course, the science fiction for which he is famed today.

It was to a house in Havelock Park, 4 Campbell Road, that Rudyard Kipling (1865-1936) and his sister, Trix, were sent to live with a foster family in 1871, while their parents lived in India. During his five and a half years of 'abandonment' Kipling suffered bullying and mental torture from the foster mother and her son. The author retained a sense of injustice and hurt about his time in Portsmouth, recalling the 'house of desolation' sixty years later. Dickens would have understood: 'In the little world in which children have their existence, whosoever brings them up, there is nothing so finely perceived and finely felt, as injustice.' His subjects and perspective make Kipling an unfashionable writer today but he was a household name and a best-selling author. He sold seven million copies of his books in Britain and eight million in the United States. He was the 'balladeer of Empire', his *Barrack Room Ballads* (1892)

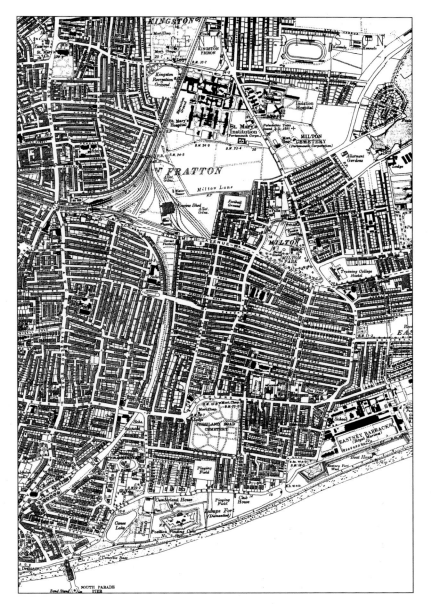

This detail from the 1933 OS map shows the route of the former East Southsea Railway. (With permission of the Ordnance Survey, NC/01/469)

used the vernacular forms of ballad and music hall songs to bring *Gunga Din* and *Mandalay* into the popular consciousness. It is strange that in the unlettered city of Portsmouth three of the most popular writers of their era had their formative experiences there and within the scope of a kilometre and over a fifteen-year period. They benefited from living in a time of a mass readership; a habit fed by the 'railway literature' supplied by the likes of W.H. Smith and its network of 1,000 railway bookstalls.

As the coming of the railway to Portsmouth boosted that town then adding a suburban branch line could surely do the same for Southsea. A plan was first mooted in 1866 and finally after a cabal of local businessmen and

Seafront shelter on the Esplanade east of Southsea Castle.

politicians pushed it through and engineered the compulsory purchase, the East Southsea Railway was opened on 1 July 1885. The line arched south from Goldsmith Avenue to a terminus at Granada Road, close to South Parade Pier. The railway may have helped housing development in the area of Festing Grove to the east of Craneswater Park's Gothic villas, but the arrival of other forms of local travel, such as the trams, meant that this line never made a profit and closed in 1914.

The focal attraction of this eastern end of the resort was South Parade Pier. The original pier had been opened in 1879 – a seamark of the resort's east end just as Clarence Pier marked the west end. This first South Parade Pier was a modest affair with two pavilions flanking an entrance to a deck that led to a small concert hall at the seaward end. In July 1904 it burnt down, a familiar occupational fate for piers. The Borough Council bought the site and decided to commission a grander replacement, choosing as their architect G.E. Smith, then in the early trials of his masterwork – the Technical Institute and Free Library. George Edwin Smith (1868-1944) is another of those under-celebrated local architectural heroes. Born in Portsmouth, educated at Portsmouth Grammar School and ten years learning his trade with Fareham and Gosport architect, William Yeardye, he set up his own practice in Southsea in 1896. As a designer he was inventive and versatile. Breweries often provided work for architects and Smith designed Gosport's Park Hotel for a small Emsworth brewery. In 1906 he completed the Reginald Road schools complex, Elementary and Infants' Schools and Instruction Centre, where the 'free Renaissance' façades managed to humanise the appearance of these Borough institutions. He designed commercial buildings – the Mikado and Victoria Buildings in Elm Grove and shops for the Portsea Co-operative Society; banks such as Lloyds in Gosport High Street, a gym

and chapels. The RN School of Physical Training in Flathouse Road has also been attributed to him. The Chapel and Superintendent's house at the Municipal Cemetery, Milton, and the Church of England's Mission Chapel of St Patrick at Eastney (now housing) were certainly designed by him. These last buildings show his individualistic response to each task and a readiness to experiment.

As this inventory shows, local architects like Smith could devote a career to making extensive individual contributions to the cityscape of one place, but its provincial status would only bring them anonymity. The South Parade Pier contract and the Municipal College gave Smith a higher profile among his contemporaries. The new pier, opened in 1908, was grander than its predecessor and reflected Edwardian enthusiasm for these 'people's palaces.' Entrance to the pier was through a glazed canopy that projected out over the esplanade. Passing shops and steamer ticket kiosks, the visitor walked into a hall dominated by the shipping office and giving onto a tea room and small concert hall. The tea room had a westerly orientation to catch the afternoon sun. The concert hall was a multi-purpose space usable as a reception hall, venue for bazaars, skating rink and so on. The pier's largest space was next door – the Pavilion Kursaal. ('Kursaal' was a fashionable and popular term at the time and is a German word for a rest room in a spa.) The main concerts and Pierrot shows were held here in an ornate galleried auditorium that offered an audience capacity of over two thousand. The higher level offered the opportunity to promenade through the Kursaal and out onto a balcony. From here the view was seaward out over an octagonal expanse of deck across a bandstand to the steamer assembly point beyond. Smith's building was designed to be an experience – an architectural promenade – and to work as a 'winter palace' as much as a summertime venue. Piers were in their heyday and it was only later, well into the twentieth century, that their appeal declined.

Piers supplied the iconic image that often fronted those 'wish you were here' postcards from the seaside. The postcard had been officially launched by the Austrian post office in 1869. When the British postcard was put on sale in October 1870, it sold 675,000 on the first day. By the 1890s most British-designed cards were printed in the German states ('chromographed in Saxony' was typical). The British postal authorities' innovation was to allow messages to be written on the address side for the first time in 1902. Postcards became both mementos and collectable and this was something which the British authorities relied on in 1944 when they issued a request through the BBC for postcards that showed images

A parade at HMS St Vincent, Gosport, 1900.

King Edward VII inspecting the fleet at a Review in 1905.

of the northern coastal areas of France as a source of topographical and strategic information for the Normandy landings.

Whatever the format, the local view subjects of beach, bandstand, pier, promenade and Kursaal predominated, yet the humorous card also has a long history, often relying on the *double entendre* to add a sexual frisson, yet beat the censor. Cards bearing a cartoon by Donald McGill, or one of his followers, suggested there might be something a bit risqué about seaside encounters. Some of the slot machines on piers and in the popular amusement arcades added to this tradition of seaside fun.

What a large town like Portsmouth could offer was spectacle, and uniquely the Fleet Review. The first official review was in 1773, although William III had come down in 1693 to cast an eye over his ships anchored at Spithead. The reviews became regularised in Queen Victoria's reign and even institutionalised. After her first official review in 1842 there was one in every remaining decade of the century and eighteen altogether from that year until 1918.

By the Review of 1845 Victoria and Albert were installed at Osborne House on the Isle of Wight, just down the coast from the port that was becoming the naval arsenal of Empire. The royal presence at these reviews brought on their coat tails the diplomatic corps, foreign royalty, MPs and the press. The direct railway link to Portsmouth made it easier for excursionists to come to these events and estimates suggest that a crowd of around 100,000 people packed the beach, ramparts and Common to witness the mock naval engagement in the Solent at the 1853 review. An invitation to the Fleet Review was often a means of honouring visitors, Sultans, potentates and crowned heads were brought to them, including the Kaiser in 1896. Queen Victoria celebrated her Golden Jubilee in 1887 and Diamond Jubilee in 1897 with reviews. The one in July 1914 was in reality a test mobilisation before the start of the hostilities in August.

The *Illustrated Guide to Southsea and Portsmouth* of 1906 shows how aware the town was that the presence of Royal Navy ships was a capital selling point. The guide's photographs engaged the holidaymaker with pictures of the illumination of the Fleet at Spithead, soldiers at Clarence Barracks, field-gun drill at Whale Island, a medal ceremony at Colewort Barracks, warships and soldiers in a Military Review on Southsea Common, and so on. The guide promised the visitor the best of both worlds: in Southsea you could have it all – solitude and sociability.

In another guide, The Southsea and Portsmouth Coronation Souvenir Guide of 1911, the towns are offered as the patriotic visitor's choice. Here were 'the finest Naval reviews in the world' with the nightly entertainment of torpedo boats, illuminated by searchlights, trying to rush the harbour entrance. Poignantly the guide included a photograph of the cruiser HMS *Hampshire* which, in 1916, hit a mine off Orkney and sank with the loss of 643 lives, among whom was Lord Kitchener – immortalised as the face on the famous 'Wanted' recruitment poster.

Guides of the time made equal play of Southsea as a summer and winter resort, and a therapeutic choice as much as anything. Statistics were quoted that claimed low rates of 'respiratory death' but high mean winter temperatures. You might have been surrounded 'by the spirits of England's heroes' but Southsea was 'very free from fogs'. The visitor could take 'sensible constitutionals' or 'play improving sports' on croquet lawns and tennis courts, on the charming golf links and at the Saxe-Weimar Bowling Club. It was also safe to drink the water – 'Portsmouth possesses the finest constant supply of pure water in the United Kingdom.' There was also a hint of something socially purer in the suburbs; 'As regards Society, it is beloved of the services, many thousands of Naval Military officers reside here with their families.' Portsmouth and Southsea certainly had a lot to offer the nineteenth-century visitor, and they came in droves.

Scene from a Fleet Review, c. *1906.*

CHAPTER 5

Victorian City

In 1812, the year HMS *Victory* returned from sea for the last time, a second child was born to Elizabeth and John Dickens on 7 February in their terraced house at Mile End. John was an assistant in the Dockyard's Navy Pay Office but in the staffing adjustments at the end of the Napoleonic war he was transferred to London and then Chatham at the start of 1815. Charles Dickens could recollect little of Portsmouth and it was London that made him as he also, to an extent, made it. His birthplace was bought by the corporation in 1904 and opened as a museum that a 1906 guide described as containing 'some interesting relics of the novelist'.

At the start of the nineteenth century Portsmouth was indisputably a company town, dominated by the Dockyard. In 1801 the town's population was 33,000 and of these 4,000 worked there. By 1901 the city of Portsmouth's population was 186,000 and by 1914 it was 245,827. War, or the threat of it, was the engine that drove this: initially the Napoleonic wars, then the reconstruction of the Dockyard to accommodate a steam navy, the demands made on the Army and Navy of a growing empire and the wars that accompanied this growth. At the end of century the city's growth was activated by the start of a new rearmament race. Yet as Portsmouth urbanised and expanded north and east, out from Portsea and the old walled town, civilian industry and trades also grew: breweries, small-scale manufacture, the corset industry and services connected with the visitor trade. The march of the bricks was gradual but inexorable. In 1815 most of Portsea Island was still open land or farmland; by the 1870s this was true of, perhaps, only two-thirds. By 1939 the built city covered virtually the whole island.

We have seen that the coming of the railway helped development but had arrived comparatively late, in 1848. An earlier transport communications project – the London to Portsmouth Canal via Arundel – had been abandoned. The purpose behind this navigation, opened in 1822, was to transport raw materials south for the Navy and carry farm produce back to London. But the scheme proved not to be financially or ecologically viable. When the project was conceived war had made the coastal trading route around Kent a hazardous one. Peace and railway competition undermined the profits forecast and the leakage of seawater into Portsmouth's water supply undermined local support. Locks at

Charles Dickens birthplace, Old Commercial Road, Landport.

Treadgolds & Co, the ironmongers, Portsea. The metal store and stock room have been preserved as a museum exhibit.

Milton are the navigation's only visible remnant. Locksway Road, Canal Walk and Arundel Street trace its route across Portsea Island.

The powerhouse of the Dockyard spawned ancillary industries. A classic example of a small-scale inner city industrial enterprise that grew and changed with urbanisation was the firm of Treadgolds. A marriage in 1781 united the Treadgold and Jones families, cabinet makers and blacksmiths respectively. Two of the in-laws formed a partnership in 1809 to begin trading as ironmongers and smiths. The firm made and sold equipment, tools and metal supplies to a wide variety of Portsea Island customers including smiths, shipwrights, wheelwrights and coopers. It also supplied horseshoe nails and moulds, ridge stays, hoes, scythes, locks, keys and bottlejacks to farriers, builders and farmers. By the late 1860s Treadgolds' cramped back street site, fronting on to Bishop Street in Portsea, was a pocket industrial complex including offices, a shop, cart store, stable yard and stables, metal store and a forge. Government contracts and agricultural tools for farmers were the mainstays of the business, but as markets and retail practices changed so the firm adapted to meet them. Early success brought upward mobility with this entrepreneurial family moving to a substantial house opposite Southsea's Canoe Lake in 1872. Commercial success was accompanied by increasing community involvement and the family became active in local improvement schemes and invested in local pier, tramway, steamship and waterworks companies. Treadgolds was the archetypal local firm and survived for almost 200 years.

If there was money in iron, so too was there in cloth. The clothing industry was a significant sector of Victorian Portsmouth's local economy, employing around 40 per cent of the manufacturing work force between 1841 and 1911. Until late in the nineteenth century all navy personnel had to buy their own uniforms, so naval tailoring provided a lucrative trade. The vagaries of naval pay and recruitment and the often cyclical nature of Dockyard employment also meant that the wives of dockies and matelots had to seek paid work. Here was a reserve army of female labour desperate for work and vulnerable to exploitation by clothing manufacturers. Warehouses supplied the materials to outworkers to be made into garments at home. One of the mainstays of this manufacture was corset making, a concern that expanded to become a major industry in the area and lasted well into he twentieth century. Homeworking and corset sweatshops continued, but by the late 1870s these were supplemented by factories, some of which were substantial industrial premises.

Substantial too were the premises of another, more visible, city industry – brewing. The dockers' industrial thirst, the run-ashore needs of the Navy coupled with a dubious water supply made beer a staple commodity in the Victorian city and the brewery towers a distinctive part of its cityscape. The brewery building programme is also now a roll call of beers now past, in an industry notoriously prone to takeovers. Among those lost are Palmer's St Pauls Steam Brewery (1869), King's Lion Brewery (1878), Jewell's Catherine Brewery (1879), Peters' Kingston Brewery (1886), Portsmouth United's Elm Brewery in Southsea (1898) and the St George's Brewery, Portsea (1890s). The latter was built for the appropriately named Lush & Co. and was in the style of the times with a decorative, arcaded façade to the brewhouse and an industrial landscape of maltings and chimneys. Brickwoods, which outlasted them all, built its brewery in 1900.

Byculla House, Kent Road, Southsea, was built in 1895 for the Brickwoods brewing family.

Charles Dickens, reputedly fond of a drink himself, recorded in his novels all types and places of drinking: David Copperfield, memorably, asks in a pub for 'a glass of the Genuine Stunning'. Most Victorian churchmen did not take a lax view of drinking and saw alcohol as a threat to moral instruction. Joseph Wigram, later to be vicar of Portsea and who died in 1878, reported on that place's moral anarchy in a letter in 1851. Prostitution was allied to the public house trade, many of which 'pander for their maintenance by female degradation'. And the clientele? The returning crews of battleships 'excited by release from long-continued restraint' and with 'accumulated wages... are the prey of the agents of Satan and carried away captive by every lust'. To Archdeacon Wigram, the absence of restraint among wild matelots and mechanics was in part due to the agencies of 'scepticism and socialism'.

Progressive Victorian churchmen looked for ways of administering pastoral influence and these increasingly took the form of urban missions in the latter part of the century. Campaigning evangelical ministries were developed by John Knapp at St John's, Portsea, in the 1850s and under Frederick Baldey at St Simon's in the 1860s. Knapp started prayer meetings, Sunday schools and the Portsea Island YMCA. His Circus Church, using a redundant circus building in Landport, highlighted the initial lack of urban churches, but by the early 1890s there were nineteen Anglican churches. Baldey established a mission hall in Albert Road and attended to welfare provision through blanket and coal societies and a soup kitchen. He was keen to foster the Band of Hope, the Scripture Union, organise beach services for visitors and, by the 1880s, host Moody and Sankey revivalist meetings.

More middle-way Anglican missions focused on the parish of St Mary's, Portsea and the urban missions of Edgar Jacob, vicar for seventeen years

St Simon's church, Waverley Road, Southsea, built by architect Thomas Hellyer, 1864-6.

St Agatha's church, Charlotte Street, was built in 1895 (architect J.H. Ball) and was used as a Navy store during the later twentieth century. It is now restored as a church and gallery.

until 1895 and then Cosmo Lang (1896-1901) who became Archbishop of Canterbury. During Jacob's stewardship a new church was built (1887-89) as a second replacement for the original early twelfth-century church where Charles Dickens had been baptised. Designed by Sir Arthur Blomfield (1829-1899) architect of St Barnabas' at Jericho in Oxford and architectural master to Thomas Hardy, this large, 2,000-capacity church resembled the 'wool churches' of East Anglia.

The Catholic missionary charge was most memorably led by Father Robert Dolling. A veteran of fieldwork in the East End of London, Dolling was the second Winchester College missioner to Landport in 1885. In a memoir of his mission, *Ten Tears in a Portsmouth Slum* he described his district, wedged between Portsea, Commercial Road and the Dockyard Wall: 'The streets are, most of them, very narrow and quaint, named after great admirals and sea-battles, with old world, red tiled roofs, and interiors almost like the cabins of ships.' He raised enough money to fund three schools, convert a redundant chapel into a gymnasium, run a mission and almshouses and finance outings and clubs. He campaigned against alcoholism and prostitution and to improve the lot of the working man and identified with ideas of wealth redistribution, land reform and free education. In his later years he publicly supported Labour leaders of the day. The monument to his mission commitment is St Agatha's church. This red-brick, Romanesque basilica was designed by Joseph Ball of Southsea and was built in one year (1895) by W.R. Light and Son of Southsea and adorned by the ornamental plastering (sgraffito) of Arts and Crafts artist Heywood Sumner.

Dickens was against the overseas missionary enterprises of the time but supported non-denominational urban missions and probably would have approved of Dolling's utilitarianism. He was critical too of the evangelical insistence on strict Sunday observance. He saw sabbatarianism as discrimination against the working class on their one day off and railed against it in journalistic pieces such as *The Sunday Screw*. Alcohol abuse may have been a social problem but it was not confined to the lower orders and public houses sometimes also served as important community institutions. Apart from offering sociability and drink, the pub in a town like Portsmouth acted as a labour exchange, especially for dock and services recruitment; a place to disburse wages, as a mail collecting point, meeting place for working men's clubs and political groups. The pub was also increasingly a place of entertainment with music hall growing out of the mid-century variety saloons; pub games also developed through the century, from skittles to billiards.

Drinking establishments ranged from bare beer houses to the surviving inns such as The George and the Dolphin in the High Street, patronised by a more bourgeois clientele. Railway Hotels met a particular need and the typical public house outgrew the beerhouse in the drive to feature entertainment. One solution was provided by the original Theatre Royal which was built on brewery land and linked by a door to the adjoining White Swan. A district like Landport, for example, comprised 1,100 houses and fifty-two public houses. As Father Dolling once observed in the 1880s, 'Oh, that bishops had the energy of the brewers'. One result of this energy was the emergence of the pub architect – a specialist in escapist interiors, able to design trademark buildings for the competitive brewer.

Late Victorian pub interiors were designed to insulate the customer from a harsh world, even if the public bar was less insulated than the saloon. So this stage-set for the theatre of everyday life came to include painted mirrors, richly-decorated glass embossed and cut, pot plants, elaborate joinery (especially the back-fittings to the bar), decorative tile work, extravagant plasterwork friezes and ceilings, china beer engine handles and decorative marble. Local examples of architects whose regular supply of jobs came from pub commissions were George Rake and his pupil, Arthur Edward Cogswell (1858-1934). Cogswell was the archtypal local architect in the late Victorian and Edwardian eras. He spent his career in Portsmouth, starting an apprenticeship with Rake at fourteen and still designing in the town in his seventieth year. He was involved in building, or remodelling, some sixty pubs and hotels. The most distinctive survivals are the Talbot, Pelham (1897) Rutland Hotels (1898), the Pompey (1898) and the Eastfield Hotel (c. 1905). The first four featured elaborate half-timbering and glazed brickwork, while the Eastfield's façades represented a complete departure into ceramics with pale-green glazed brick upper walls and dark green faience for the ground floor. All have distinctive skylines and the Talbot has a gambrel-roofed (witches' hat) turret.

Pub work represented regular work for the practice but Cogswell could and did turn his hand to anything. An inventory of his completed buildings includes the neo-Flemish Renaissance Highland Road Schools, offices for Portsmouth Water Company, Morant's Store in Southsea, Kingston Cemetery Gateway, the Evening News building, Francis Avenue Schools, St Paul's Drill Hall for the 2nd Hants Artillery Volunteers, the red-brick, Tudor/Gothic Guardians and Registrar's offices, Milton Schools, the 'Tyrolean Tudor' Brickwoods residence, Byculla House, the Turret Hotel and Lennox Mansions, the Edwardian Baroque Carnegie Free Library in Fratton, St Saviour's church in Stamsham and the North-West Frontier Palace Cinema, with its Islamic motifs. Cogswell made a prodigious impact on how Portsmouth looks today. With George Rake, A.E. Cogswell, G.E. Smith and the suitably named Vernon Inkpen, there should be enough for a 'Portsmouth School', if only their styles were not so eclectic.

During his apprenticeship Cogswell was involved in the drawings and work for two projects: Kingston gaol and the new lunatic asylum, completed in 1877 and 1879 respectively. Before the building of Kingston, the Borough gaol had been in Penny Street in Portsmouth's old town. As the Industrial Revolution gathered pace in the early decades of the nineteenth century, imprisonment was the main form of punishment, that and the parallel 'solution' of transportation. In the early years of the century Portsmouth gaol saw a rise in the number of committals, especially those convicted of naval desertion, smuggling or being 'disorderly women'.

Prison reform measures tried to eradicate the overcrowded, lock-up bedlams of former times; from 1816 the insane could be removed to a lunatic asylum and the 1823 Gaol Act talked of the need to provide education and religious instruction. Throughout the nineteenth century

The former Turret Hotel and Lennox Mansions in Clarence Parade, designed by A.E. Cogswell, 1896.

The Talbot in Goldsmith Avenue, designed by architect, A.E. Cogswell.

hard labour was a common punishment. Portsmouth became a centre where prisoners were used as labourers on public works and convict work gangs became a familiar sight in the city. When real work couldn't be found, then the treadmill or the crank were substituted. Portsmouth installed a treadmill in 1832 and ran it for six hours a day. In 1860 the gaol installed partitions to stop association between prisoners. Others advocated the Separate System where prisoners were kept locked in the solitude of their cells to contemplate their mistaken paths. Portsmouth gaol experimented with this, keeping boys and women prisoners isolated in cells, picking oakum (the highly tedious and difficult job of taking apart old rope for recycling). Another prison was built close to the Dock police station in 1853-54, designed for those awaiting transportation or serving long sentences who had previously been incarcerated in the floating hulks.

A look at the crime figures in Portsmouth for the mid-nineteenth century paints a picture of the times. Of all the indictable offences known to the police between 1858 and 1875, 82 per cent were larceny offences – theft of clothing or watches to sell in pawn brokers and dolly shops, or theft of food and drink. Portsea farms were a target: one case involved four juveniles, aged twelve to fifteen, sentenced to a month's hard labour each for stealing potatoes. In May 1850 six boys were spotted picking apples from the garden of William Horner; the three caught each received fourteen days' hard labour. Persistent pickpockets could receive draconian sentences such as transportation and, until 1808, the death penalty. Most of those sentenced to hang in the 1820s were property offenders and it wasn't until 1861 that the death penalty was confined to murder, high treason, arson in HM Dockyards and violent piracy. Charles Dickens became involved in the debates about capital punishment and after witnessing an execution in 1840 became an abolitionist. Hanging as a public spectacle was not ended until 1868. Twelve murders were recorded in the Portsmouth Police District in the seventeen years between 1858 and 1875.

There was no social safety net for those who were destitute or otherwise socially disadvantaged but the authorities were much exercised by the problem of vagrancy. The Vagrancy Act of 1824, designed for the 'Punishment of Idle and Disorderly Persons and Rogues and Vagabonds', created a catch-all which targeted the people so described but could also include sailors seeking ships, 'shallow coves' (destitute sailors), run-away young people, the itinerant unemployed, service widows and deserted women. In 1831 a private female penitentiary was set up in Portsmouth's St Vincent Street for penitent women who had 'departed from the paths of virtue'. Those less penitent were charged as 'disorderly prostitutes' and could be sentenced to two weeks' or more hard labour. 'Disorderly' here often meant using obscene language. In 1864 the Contagious Diseases Act was introduced to apply to garrison towns such as Portsmouth and gave the Metropolitan Police, whose jurisdiction was the Dockyard, the power to refer suspect women for medical examination. Infected women were then committed to the locked wards of the local hospital or workhouse for treatment. Some Portsmouth women were referred back to magistrates for absconding from hospital or for riotous behaviour while there.

Child poverty was a major problem in Victorian Britain and Portsmouth had its share. In the middle decades of the century some of the poorest areas of Portsmouth, the old town and parts of Landport and Portsea, families lived in poorly built back-to-backs. In some courts one tap and one privy served sixty people and an open drain ran through the courtyard. The military requirement to keep the gates of the old town shut overnight caused local difficulty because the rank night waggons with their cargoes from the cesspits were confined there until morning. Diets were poor and adulteration of food a common practice. Outbreaks of smallpox and typhus were frequent and the cholera epidemics of 1848-49 and 1853-54 cut swathes through these communities. A Board of Public Health investigation by Robert Rawlinson reported in 1848 that 20 per cent of infants did not live beyond their first year. The local annual death rate for children under five was 8 per cent.

For those poorest children who did survive the hazards of early childhood, the prospects of receiving much of an education were equally poor. Before the 1870 Education Act, the state's first attempt to ensure elementary educational for all, education provision was a patchwork of charity schools, dame schools (mostly daytime child-minding), private foundations, such as the Royal Seamen's and Marines' Orphan School and Church of England and Nonconformist schools, with their monitorial systems, where the teachings of one instructor was passed on to the rest of the school through the older pupils. An example of the latter was the Portsea Beneficial School.

One inspiring beacon in this otherwise gloomy story of poor children was the example of John Pounds. Born in Portsmouth in 1766, the son of a Dockyard sawyer, he became a shipwright apprentice at twelve but suffered a disabling fall into a dry dock two years later. He spent the years needed for recovery in self-education; and when later he set up in business as a cobbler in Portsea's St Mary's Street, he turned his workshop into an informal community centre, reading and drafting letters for the illiterate and taking street children into his shopfront 'school'. After his death in 1839 lithograph copies of a drawing of this 'gratuitous Teacher of Poor Children' at work gained wide distribution. One of these was spotted by Dr Thomas Guthrie of Edinburgh who investigated Pounds' story and inspired by it, went on to found the Ragged Schools, designed to give

poor children a free practical education. By 1870 there were 350 schools in London and the provinces, providing education and challenging the State to do more.

Remedy and reform came from the government and from community self-help. In December 1872 thirty people at a public meeting agreed to set up a local co-operative and in May 1873 the Portsea Island Mutual Co-operative Society's first shop opened in Charles Street, Landport. The principles of democracy, community responsibility and mutuality were applied to the food retail trade.

The 1845 Sewage and Drainage of Towns Act called upon commissioners to do something about their own facilities. Portsmouth Borough Council acted fifteen years later. A sanitary authority was set up and a rate levied. Four years after that, in 1864 the Borough Engineer put forward a scheme for underground sewers converging on an outfall at the mouth of Langstone Harbour. There was a topographical difficulty; parts of the island were so low-lying that a pump would be needed to bring the waste up to a higher level sewer prior to discharge. A pumping station was built at Eastney in 1868, but the town's growth and shoreline pollution that resulted demanded more effective technology. In 1886 the new machinery arrived at Eastney in the form of two Clayton and two James Watt reciprocating compound condensing beam engines.

In the same year that these machines began their task, building work started on that essential nineteenth-century symbol of civic maturity – a new town hall. An expeditionary working party was dispatched north to look for a suitable model and designer. The architect chosen was William Hill of Leeds who produced a design not unlike his town hall at Bolton which in turn had been influenced by Cuthbert Broderick's town hall at Leeds. Opened in 1890, the resulting Italianate, Classical building featured a front façade dominated by a dramatic staircase leading to two huge entrance doors under a Corinthian portico, topped with a statue of Neptune. The town hall introduced a sort of municipal opera into the streetscape!

The Reform Act of 1884 began the process of improving Parliamentary representation to better reflect the population shift to the towns but the electorate was largely the propertied, ratepayers, long-term lodgers, and skilled workers, but not all of these. Until the Representation of the People Act, in 1918, only around 60 per cent of the adult males in Porstmouth, and none of the women, had the vote.

In the period up to 1918 the Liberals and Conservatives who were elected to the two-member seat of Portsmouth were drawn from a narrow range of predictable backgrounds. In the 1900 'Khaki Election', called during the Boer War, both elected members were Conservatives from military backgrounds. Other Conservative MPs from the 1910 and

1916 elections included two navy men – Lord Charles Beresford and Sir Hedworth Meux, respectively. Charles Beresford was the second son of the 4th Earl of Waterford, Commander of the Channel Fleet and had spent a time as aide-de-camp to Queen Victoria. His supporters knew where they stood and the editor of the *Portsmouth Times*, in a sweeping endorsement of his election, cast him as the politician 'ready to rescue Britannia from the foes who are menacing her life with their discredited nostrums of socialism, Free Trade, Disestablishment, Disendowment, Home Rule, Reduced Armaments and attacks on capitalism.' Sir Hedworth Meux, the second son of the Earl of Durham, had been Commander-in-Chief, Portsmouth and the China Squadron, aide-de-camp to King Edward VII and commander of the Royal Yacht, retiring as Admiral of the Fleet. *The Hampshire Telegraph* tried to put their deference into verse:

> The voice you long have used in command
> Use still, and Portsmouth will behind you stand.

From his experience as a parliamentary reporter, Charles Dickens had concluded that the House of Commons, as the 'best club in London', was an ineffective legislature. As a progressive reformer he had no time for Tories – 'people whom, politically, I despise and abhor'. Dickens' attitudes towards women's issues was more ambivalent, even contradictory. He did not subscribe to women's rights and his preference was for women as domestic homemakers; through his fiction he exposed such scandals as the sewing outwork system. In his journalism Dickens railed against the exploitation of servants but he retained them in real life. He championed legal changes to make divorce easier and affordable but kept a mistress himself.

The election of 1918 saw the first woman stand for a Portsmouth parliamentary seat – a Liberal candidate, Alison Garland. Her platform included a comprehensive housing programme, the setting up of a Ministry of Health, Home Rule for Ireland and self-determination for India. The years just before the First World War had seen the Suffragist campaign at its most intense and yet caught between the perennial dilemmas of militancy and restraint. The more militant WSPU (Women's Social and Political Union) had favoured direct action, confrontation, hunger strikes. They seized newspaper and public attention. The less militant NUWSS (National Union of Women's Suffrage Societies) built a base, organized demonstrations and lobbied. Both pressure groups had branches in Portsmouth and in July 1913 the NUWSS had organised a march from Portsmouth to London. It frequently met with a militant reaction en route. However, women's war work, notable locally in the hostile, male environment of Portsmouth Dockyard, made the case for votes for women politically inevitable after the war and the franchise was extended to women over thirty in 1918. If Britannia had been a British citizen before 1918 she wouldn't have had the vote!

So long as the city air didn't kill you, it could make you free. In spite of remaining class barriers, the city held out prospects and you could see people who had advanced. Tradition was loosening its hold and you could learn the urban way of life. One place for this was the park. The need for urban parks had been officially recognised by a Parliamentary Select Committee in 1833 that had promoted their elevating influences; places 'to train and educate the people to neatness in dress, habit of order, and respectability of conduct and behaviour.' So these arenas of rational recreation could also be places of improvement where classes might meet and learn from each other. Some municipal parks, such as Liverpool's Sefton and Stanley Parks became other landscapes that contradicted the surrounding city: boating lakes, boathouses, lodges, pagodas, palm houses, shelters, bandstands. Southsea Common and the seafront most resembled this in Portsmouth, but Victoria Park was to come closer to the archetypal municipal garden.

When it was first conceived in 1878, Victoria Park's site was bisected by a railway line with a pleasure ground to the north and a recreation ground to the south. The northern part was guarded by a lodge, with a bandstand as its central focal point. Public performances of music were seen as having a socialising, even moral, influence. During the Imperial era, the park became a repository of campaign and campaigner memorials, either sited there deliberately or relocated to avoid some road or urban improvement scheme. Park layout was susceptible to changing fashions in gardening. When Victoria Park opened massed bedding plants were fashionable and the beds next to the entrance gates were laid out in the form of the borough coat of arms. There were issues over Sunday use and discussions about appropriate park games and norms of behaviour. Parks were subject to regulations and park-keepers, but the municipal park provided that rarity in Victorian cities – freely accessible public space.

If parks were institutions of improvement, so were Friendly Societies and working men's clubs. Towards the end of the century organised leisure came in the form of cycling clubs and sports like football which started to become institutionalised. The impetus for this often came from the brewing trade; brewers John Peters and John Brickwood with architect Alfred Bone and others founded Portsmouth Football Club as a professional club in 1898.

Theatre and music hall flourished and by the end of the first decade of the twentieth century Portsmouth had two significant theatres both designed by Frank Matcham (1854-1920); designer of 150 theatres around the country, including the London Coliseum, and both Brighton and Bristol Hippodromes. He was the doyen of theatre architects. His transformation of Portsmouth's Theatre Royal created an auditorium space fit for Beerbohm Tree, Sarah Bernhardt, Lily Langtry, Henry Irving and Ellen Terry, all of whom appeared there. In 1907 Matcham was commissioned to build a theatre specifically for Southsea and the Kings was the result. This theatre survives today as veritable time capsule of an Edwardian theatre and a model of society at the time – its design shows great attention was paid to the class of its clientele, just as the three classes of railway compartment or pub's saloon and public bars did in those spheres. The artisan 'hoi polloi' sat on benches in the vertigo-inducing upper gallery, while the moneyed bourgeoisie sat on the plush seats of the cantilevered first tier, the dress circle. The theatre was consciously segregated with eleven entrances, each with its own box office.

The Theatre Royal was remodelled by Frank Matcham in 1900.

The Victoria era ended with Queen Victoria's death at Osborne House on 22 January 1901. She was carried from Cowes to Portsmouth aboard the Royal Yacht *Alberta*, steaming through lines formed by over forty battleships, whose bands played funeral marches by Chopin and Beethoven. The next day, the 2 February, two trains left Portsmouth carrying the coffin and funeral party. From Victoria station the cortège processed through the London streets to Paddington station. At Windsor two horses pulling the gun carriage kicked over the traces and realising the potential danger to the accompanying Kaiser and half of European royalty, it was decided to dispense with the restive team. The naval honour guard from HMS *Excellent* were put in harness to pull the gun carriage to Windsor Castle chapel.

Victoria was soon to be represented by a stern stone figure in many townscapes throughout the land and become an adjective to describe a morality, an era, a set of values, and its architecture. Charles Dickens had died in 1870, his death hastened, it has been said, by his intense mesmeric public readings of the Death of Nancy. He hated Victorian funeral customs and claimed that on occasions he had left funerals for fear of laughing out loud; he refused to 'endure being dressed up by an undertaker as part of his trade show'. The writer and art critic John Ruskin wrote about Dickens that he was 'a pure modernist – a leader of the steam-whistle party par excellence.' If Dickens' hero was 'essentially the ironmaster', then he had sided with the bringer of the urban industrial society. Railways had been the prime mover in the creation of modern towns like Portsmouth and would continue to be so transporting its coal, beer, newspapers, migrants, excursionists, football supporters, mail, embarking troops and evacuees.

CHAPTER 6

Imperial Fort

'Soldiers and sailors swarm towards a fort defended by sepoys.' This is a Royal Naval Museum exhibit – a diorama of an attack on an Indian fort. The model depicts an episode during the Indian Mutiny of 1857, just one of the myriad military episodes that took place during the nineteenth-century years of the British Empire. The scale and scope of the Empire meant that British governments had a worldwide remit. The logistics of policing the world required a global structure of barracks, forts, naval stations, ports, railheads, legations and coaling stations.

At its zenith in the early years of the twentieth century the British Empire nominally comprised one fifth of the world's land mass (about $11\frac{1}{2}$ million square miles). In 1910 King George V was ruler of a domain with a population of 410 million people living in self-governing dominions or in crown colonies and dependencies that were administered through the India Office, the Foreign Office or the Admiralty. Competition between European powers, local aspirations and local rivalries meant there were constant wars, skirmishes, uprisings and border disputes that prompted British punitive expeditions and gunboat diplomacy. An Army and a Navy were needed to keep the peace, show the flag and conduct wars and Portsmouth was pivotal in this whole enterprise. Defence or war spending was a familiar contentious issue and by the end of the nineteenth century some of the colonies were making direct contributions toward the operating cost of the Navy. Yet there was another problem and this involved the balance between the resources devoted to far-flung garrisons and their connecting supply lines and the defence of Metropolitan shores. Surrogate struggles might be fought between European rivals overseas but there was always a potential threat to the mother country's own 'backyard' and to its premier Imperial depot of Portsmouth.

By the early 1850s Portsmouth's defences were fragmentary and in part obsolete. The fortification line on the western shore approach to Portsmouth Harbour was about to be strengthened with an up-dating of Fort Monckton and a new fort at Gilkicker; two new polygonal forts would be built by 1858 at Gomer at Stokes Bay overlooking the Solent and at Elson near the upper Gosport shore of Portsmouth harbour. Three more forts were planned, Brockhurst, Rowner and Grange, to complete a defensive line between Gomer and Elson; Fort Blockhouse guarded the

Fort Brockhurst, Gosport.

Gosport side of the Harbour mouth. On the Portsmouth side, running along the shore south-eastwards, were some Tudor fortifications but mostly the defence works had been put in place by de Gomme in the late seventeenth century. Southsea Castle had been 'reformed' between 1813 and 1816 to provide accommodation for 200 men, better platforms for larger guns and a remodelled seaward-facing battery. Lumps 'Fort' battery (subject to sea erosion) was the only fortification between the Castle and the Fort at the south-eastern most tip of Portsea island. This was Fort Cumberland. Built initially with earthen ramparts in the last decade of the seventeenth century in response to France's maritime expansionist aims of the 1670s and '80s, it was at the time England's strongest fortress. This was replaced over a thirty-year period from 1780 with a stone and brick fort built by prisoner labour and designed by John Desmaretz, Clerk in Ordinary to the Chief Engineer. The decision to rebuild was prompted by twenty years of fearfulness about the French invasion threat after the Seven Years' War (1756-63).

Along the northern edge of Portsea Island ran Hilsea Lines, ramparts constructed from Portsdown-quarried chalk blocks and with earth merlons, or parapets, protecting gun casements. Their main function in the early nineteenth century had been to delay the arrival of the railway. Anyone approaching these forts and defences would have approached over the glacis, the outer slope beyond the moat; beneath their feet could have been a counterscarp gallery used to pour enfilading fire at anyone in the moat. This gallery would have been reached by a bomb-proof tunnel, or caponier; ahead would have been the bastions projecting towards them from the ramparts; the tapering channels cut into these would have signalled embrasures for cannons. Ravelin, berm, enceinte, salient, banquette, the terre-plein and redan all contrived to suggest what was here – a different world.

The British had been slow to recognise the inevitable need to convert the wood and sail navy into a steam navy. Once they did the nautical technology race with the French was joined. Even though the two countries had been on the same side in the Crimean War (1853-56) against the Russians, from across the Channel most French actions were interpreted as potentially hostile or expansionist. So the construction of a new arsenal and dockyard at Cherbourg naval base during the 1850s had to be seen in that light. There was jockeying for diplomatic status but the true intentions of Napoleon III and his government towards Britain were difficult to read. Certainly there were large sections of the population in both countries that mistrusted the old enemy. At the end of the 1850s two developments in miltary technology increased this international paranoia. In 1858 the British engineer William Armstrong successfully produced a heavy rifled, breech loading cannon with greater penetration and range – doubling the notional range to 8,000 yards. Although initially this gave great military benefit, it also meant that other nations would soon seek similar advantages and once this was achieved, neither the Hilsea Lines nor the line of Gosport forts could protect Portsmouth Harbour from bombardment. Equally the harbour was more vulnerable to attack from warships in the Solent.

This seaborne threat was given added menace by another development – the ironclad ship. This was an area of maritime technology where Britain had innovated but not developed. France had persisted and built. By the early 1860s France had launched the first sea-going ironclad, *La*

Gloire, a ship that immediately made other warships outdated. A few years earlier a civil service committee had been set up to investigate the two countries' naval strengths. The report's conclusion about Britain's comparatively high proportion of naval ships being dispersed across the globe to Empire stations gave pause for thought. Details of the impending French lead in ironclads prompted action. An ironclad programme to outbuild the French was embarked on and the sitting Royal commission on the National Defences included the protection of Portsmouth in its remit. The Commission reported in February 1860. Briefly, it concluded: a fully-manned Channel protection fleet would be too expensive; the size of a field army available to meet any invading force would be small, particularly as a sizeable proportion of regular army troops were on colonial duties abroad. So the answer was forts. Crimean veterans recalled the Russian sea forts protecting the naval base at Kronstadt. Versions of these should be built out in the Solent at Spithead to protect that anchorage and the Dockyard. Forts were also needed to the west of the existing Gosport forts and along Portsdown Hill.

In the ensuing Cabinet battle over cost, Spithead and Gosport forts were omitted from the plan. In private Prime Minister Palmerston clashed with his Chancellor, Gladstone. Palmerston wanted the amended plan to go ahead; Gladstone didn't believe in the French threat and thought the plan ill-judged, wanting rather to cut public expenditure and income tax. He threatened to resign and this move was supposed to have occasioned Palmerston's remark to Queen Victoria that it would be better to lose Mr Gladstone than to lose Portsmouth. Opposition continued from more pacific internationalists who agreed with Gladstone and from within the Services who thought the navy should be built up, turning the debate into one of ships versus forts. The debate fumed on but building work began in 1862.

The Portsdown forts were finished in the early 1870s; sitting low in the landscape, with virtually no profile, these polygonal forts were 'state of the art' Victorian technology. Problems with finding secure foundations and avoiding quicksand meant that the Solent forts were not completed until 1880. In the interim France had fought a losing war with Prussia and Napoleon had been forced into exile, in England. A generation who knew nothing of the events surrounding their inception dubbed the collective of forts, 'Palmerston's folly'. Whatever the verdict Portsmouth was left with a unique defining border landscape.

Given the city's increasing role as a military staging post for Empire, the visible presence of the army, resident and in transit, was an important part of the nineteenth-century cityscape and this increasingly took on a built form. Census records suggest that between 1851 and 1911 the armed services represented between a fifth and a quarter of the working population of Portsmouth. The seventeenth- and eighteenth-century barracks had been an improvement on encampments and the billeting of troops in pubs and civilian lodgings, but these were now inadequate. So a barracks building programme was initiated. The Royal Artillery Barracks at Hilsea was ready in 1854, Cambridge Barracks in the High Street in 1856, St George's Barracks, Gosport in 1859, the Royal Marine Barracks at Eastney in 1867 and the Victoria and the Clarence Barracks in the late 1880s.

Some demolition, including the original Theatre Royal building, preceded the construction of Cambridge Barracks with its late Regency style yellow brick façades and ceremonial three-arched entrance off the High Street. These buildings formed part of a barracks township that would by the 1890s encompass three-quarters of a city block, bounded

Portchester castle: the Norman keep.

Guildhall showing the pediment to the portico and the statue of Neptune.

South Parade Pier – a truncated version of the Edwardian pier designed by G.E. Smith in 1908.

A fragment of Bernard de Gomme's Long Curtain Battery, built in the 1680s, looking across the waters of the harbour toward Fort Blockhouse on the Gosport side.

The tram terminus at Pembroke Gardens, the approach road to Clarence Pier, early 1900s.

Contemporary Clarence Pier landscape.

The Avenue, Victoria Park, c. *1910.*

Commercial Road, Landport.

Commercial Road, Landport, early 1900s.

Naval figure in the Royal Navy war memorial to those lost at sea, Southsea Common.

Looking across the new Spur Redoubt landscaping, to the Harbour mouth and tower blocks on the Gosport shore.

Part of Thomas Ellis Owen's Sussex Terrace, Southsea.

Terraced house, Southsea, built in the early 1900s.

St Jude's Close, Southsea; 'picturesque Gothic' from 1858 by T.E. Owen.

Edwardian terraced house in Devonshire Avenue, Southsea.

Wimborne Junior School, Milton, built originally in 1875 and extended in 1906.

Milton Cross school, built in 2000.

The Shepherd's Crook, Goldsmith Avenue, built in 1914 to the design of A.E. Cogswell.

The Eastfield Hotel, Prince Albert Road, built in 1906 to the design of A.E. Cogswell.

The Harbour and Semaphore Tower.

The upper deck of HMS Warrior moored at the citadel.

Gunwharf Quays - waterfront retail and leisure development opened in 2001 on the site of the former HMS Vernon.

HM Dockyard - the Mast Pond to the former Boathouse No.6 (1843) is now converted to house an audio-visual presentation of today's Navy, opened in 2001, called 'Action Stations'.

Treadgold & Co., ironmongers, established in Bishop Street, Portsea in 1809, is now preserved as an industrial heritage museum.

The causeway across the moat to Fort Brockhurst, Gosport, built 1858-62.

The Trimast sculpture erected just north of Tipner Bridge in 2001. (Photograph by Peter Langdown, courtesy of Headley Greentree and Portsmouth and Southeast Hampshire Partnership)

Tipner Bridge masts and illuminations in 2001. (Photograph by Peter Langdown, courtesy of Headley Greentree and Portsmouth and Southeast Hampshire Partnership)

by the High Street, Pembroke Road, Victoria Avenue and three terraces and Alexandra (later Museum) Road. The original Cambridge Barracks' soldiers carried out defensive duties in Portsmouth's forts and bastions and at one time the garrison came from the Duke of Connaught's Own Hampshire Regiment which also supplied officer mercenaries for the Confederate army during the American Civil War. The only major building to survive from the other two neighbouring barracks was the north block of Clarence Barracks (named after the ubiquitous one-time Governor of Portsmouth, Colonel Fitzclarence). This former regimental institute was housed in a building inspired by a seventeenth-century French chateau, characterised by conical turreted towers.

These barracks were designed to impress but also designed to 'contain' their inmates. They were 'total institutions' and, like prisons, they encompassed separate worlds with their own regimes, unfamiliar to the surrounding civilian population. Eastney Royal Marine Barracks was a typical example of this parallel society. Fully operational in 1867, its main barrack block faced the sea across a drill square, and backed onto a drill shed, detention quarters, swimming bath and theatre (later a cinema). The field officers' quarters, Teapot Row, backed onto tennis and croquet lawns. The wooden Crinoline Church – originally designed as a Crimean war field hospital – supplied a place of worship. A giant brick water tower provided water and monumental landmark. It is possible to catch a glimpse of the more tropical-style Empire barracks by taking the Gosport ferry. Rumour had it that the long-verandahed main block on St George's south site had been intended for an overseas posting but the plans were mixed up with those for the Gosport project! Error could also account for the amazing opulence of the Eastney Barracks Officers'

St George's Barracks, Gosport, North Site, built in the late 1850s. The now redundant site awaits its fate.

HMS Warrior – *upper deck.*

Mess. A civil servant, so the story goes, added a nought to the estimate and this went unnoticed by the Admiralty. The Italian marble fireplaces and the bootneck baroque furnishings created an interior suitable for the entertaining of dignitaries including, on one occasion, the Kaiser.

The Anglesey Infantry transit barracks, built just before the Crimean War, next to the Dockyard, was taken over by the Navy in 1895, remodelled and opened as HMS *Victory* (later *Nelson*) in 1903. The Navy was slow to remodel itself after the Great French war. Napoleon Bonaparte had finally been defeated in June 1815; that was also the same month that the first steamship had visited Portsmouth. But peace brought one of those periodic downturns in naval strategic planning and the advent of the steam warship was postponed. Technological innovation continued anyway: paddle-steamers gave way to screw propulsion; the French navy introduced the explosive shell in 1837 and we have seen that their first ironclad warship followed, twenty years later. The British Navy reacted to some of these developments rather than anticipated them, but the reaction to the ironclad was immediate and took the form of HMS *Warrior*. The ship's keel was laid down in May 1859 and she was launched in December 1860.

Charles Dickens witnessed the launch; he described her as 'a black, vicious, ugly customer' but recognised her significance as the coming thing in naval warfare. The ship's coal-carrying capacity gave a range of 1,000 miles and introduced new logistical requirements into naval planning. Below decks conditions for the crew, eating and sleeping in messes between the guns, were reminiscent of shipboard life on Nelson's *Victory*. Yet ten of the guns they lived with – Armstrong breech-loading 110-pounders – signalled a major leap forward in naval gunnery. That and the arrival of the on-board engineer, flagged up the need for proficiency and naval professionalism in a new area of expertise.

Developments within the Dockyard signalled the industrialisation of defence: an iron foundry (1854), the smithy with its giant steam hammer, a steam basin of 7 acres and a 600ft-long steam factory – the Dockyard's first fireproof workshop – all testified to the arrival of a steam-powered

A mess table on HMS Warrior.

navy. After the mid-1860s the great extension of the Dockyard, annexing 86 acres of existing land and new land reclaimed from the harbour, created a 22-acre repairing basin along with machines and constructions found only in such a place; the 'Goliath' steam dredger, steam gantry cranes used in dock construction, swan-necked cranes and a floating dock repair facility (1912). The travelling steam dredgers loaded excavated mud into wagons that travelled on the Dockyard's own railway to build the substratum of the man-made Whale Island off Stamshaw. After thirty years of accumulation the island comprised 80 acres. Dug clay was also used to make bricks. Twenty million bricks a year were made by convicts, handily imprisoned just beyond the Dockyard wall.

For much of the nineteenth century a life in the Navy continued to be insecure and harsh. After the 1815 demobilisation, officers were on the beach on half pay, crews were paid off. Significant recruitment of sons from naval families as officer cadets confirmed the caste-like status of the Senior Service's upper echelons. The Crimean War had highlighted a problem with attracting enough recruits for the other ranks. Discipline could be harsh; flogging as a punishment during peacetime was only suspended in 1871 and during wartime in 1879. Service in the Imperial Navy usually resulted in long commissions in foreign parts and could involve important but seemingly inglorious tasks such as hydrography (marine surveying) or anti-slaver patrolling in the South Atlantic. In 1870, 91 of the 113 fully commissioned ships were on foreign stations.

Welfare for 'blue jackets' mostly came from private initiative. This type of effort was personified by Agnes ('Aggie') Weston, an evangelical Christian campaigner who succeeded in establishing a network of temperance hostels, Royal Sailors' Rests, from 1876. The Portsmouth Royal Sailors' Rest opened in Commercial Road in 1881. Internal service conditions had to change. The Navy had traditionally disregarded barracks ashore, and relied on accommodation afloat, using two or three-deckers as depots or receiving ships. Navy medicine, once in the vanguard, was a neglected practice. Engineers, artificers and the stokers, who toiled unseen in the stokehold infernoes, found recognition difficult to come by. Portsmouth's Royal Naval College apart, most naval education and training was done on board floating hulks.

In 1881 a Naval Medical School was set up at Haslar with improved pay and prospects for medical officers. A Royal Naval Engineering College was opened at Devonport and engineers awarded better status; there were almost 26,000 of them by 1900. As the men and the training came in from the hulks, the new facility of Whale Island, created from dredging spoil, was added to the Navy's archipelago and from 1891 became the principal gunnery school of the Royal Navy – its first shore training establishment.

Just to the north, off Tipner Point, two islands, Great Horsea and Little Horsea, were made into one to form an experimental torpedo range for the Navy in 1885; in 1909 this also became home to a Marconi wireless telegraphy station. Convicts from Kingston Prison were detailed for the landscaping work and lived on site for two and a half years in a hut encampment.

Some impetus for modernisation and change in the Navy came through journalism and popular culture. The campaigning journalist W.T. Stead wrote a series of articles for the *Pall Mall Gazette* in 1884, called 'The Truth About the Navy', which exposed the service's under-financing. Gilbert and Sullivan's *HMS Pinafore* didn't help as it poked fun at the Navy with its lampooning libretto, 'Stick close to your desks and never go to sea, And you all may be Rulers of the Queen's Navee.' The Navy felt the need to organise a major exhibition about the service in 1891 which generated huge public interest.

The bearded 'bluejacket', familiarly displayed on the packet of John Player's Navy Cut cigarettes, originated from HMS *Excellent* and reflected an 1869 Admiralty Circular which had permitted the growing of beards.

The outbreak of the First World War seemed the inevitable outcome of years of international paranoia and imperial rivalry. The final rush to mobilisation was the end-game of an arms race between the great European powers. Portsmouth had already been the locale for a significant ratcheting up of the cycle of Anglo-German naval competitiveness, culminating in the launch of the first Dreadnought in 1906. The city had also played host to one of the chief engineers of the conflagration – Kaiser Wilhelm II. A grandson of Queen Victoria, he had first visited the naval base as a boy, travelled with the Queen's funeral party from Osborne and sailed competitively with his uncle Edward VII at Cowes. He developed an ambition to match the British Navy and the Dreadnought launch had caused rethink and imitation in Germany's warship building programme. The Kaiser sailed to Portsmouth in November 1907 aboard his royal yacht, the *Hohenzollern*, with its escort squadron of battleships to attend the Fleet Review.

The Mayor of Portsmouth greeted him at the railway jetty and German sailors enjoyed free theatre trips and received concessionary free use of Corporation trams. As late as May 1913 the Kaiser and King George V were photographed riding together at Potsdam; members of the lodge of European royalty. Fifteen months later Britain and Germany were at war and the Kaiser was soon demonised as 'the beast of Berlin'.

The Dreadnought story goes back at least to 1904 and involves shipbuilding ingenuity and prowess, the radical shake-up of the Royal Navy with the politics of the Senior Service exposed to public scrutiny and an international battleship building race. Germany was accelerating her expansion as a major

PT exercises on the upper deck, c. 1900.

industrial nation and began to harbour larger mercantile ambitions. Kaiser Wilhelm II wanted to expand Germany's navy and had already found a text and an admiral to support this project. In 1890 an American captain Alfred Thayer Mahan had published a treatise *The Influence of Sea Power on History* that asserted: 'The due use and control of the sea is but one link in the chain of exchange by which wealth accumulates: but it is the central link.' The book became an international bestseller and the Kaiser was familiar with it; 'It is on board all my ships.' Another enthusiast was Rear Admiral Alfred von Tirpitz whom the Kaiser made Secretary of State of the Imperial Naval Office in 1897. His brief was to match and even challenge Britain's naval capability.

Britain's Navy, we have seen, was being accused of stagnation and underfunding. A key figure in the impetus required for reform was John Arbuthnot ('Jacky') Fisher (1841-1920). Born in Ceylon into a coffee planter's family, he joined the Royal Navy as a cadet at thirteen. He served on HMS *Victory* and HMS *Warrior*, became captain of HMS *Excellent*, the Navy's gunnery school, Director of Naval Ordnance and Torpedoes, Admiral Superintendent at Portsmouth Dockyard and became, in 1904, First Sea Lord, von Tirpitz's opposite number. Dynamic, purposeful and with the energetic perseverance, he was a strange mix of careerist and maverick (his hobbies were given as dancing and listening to sermons). His achievements as a modernizer were significant. He democratised the system of officer entry, attended to the welfare of the lower deck, closed imperial dockyards around the world and raised the profile of the navy's engineering branch, scrapped outmoded warships and pushed through a warship building programme for destroyers, submarines, new battle cruisers and a singular new type of battleship, the Dreadnought.

He was not alone in this ambition. The construction boards and admiralties of Japan, Russia and the United States had similar drawing board versions. Italian naval architect, Vittorio Cuniberti, had offered a blueprint of such a ship to his government in 1902 and when they declined he brought his designs to the attention of Portsmouth resident Fred Jane (1865-1916), who was the publisher of the annual register of ships in commission and an important voice in technical naval journalism. *Jane's Fighting Ships* of 1903 included sketches of Cuniberti's design, accompanied by the article, 'An Ideal Battleship for the British Fleet'. Fisher could rely on the far-sighted support of the Admiralty Committee on Designs, on the work of naval architect J.H. Narbeth and Chief Constructor at Portsmouth William Gard, and on the royal patronage of Edward VII; but it was his personal drive that saw it through. Amid some secrecy, 3,000 construction workers toiled through eleven and a half hour days, six days a week to ensure the first Dreadnought was ready for launch eighteen weeks after being laid down – an advance on the usual sixteen months. Eight months later the ship was fitted out and ready to undergo sea trials. This achievement made Portsmouth then the most productive dockyard in the world.

Everything was changed. At a stroke all other battleships, including Britain's, were obsolescent. German battleship building stopped as von Tirpitz absorbed the implications of the revolutionary new design. Fisher then set in train another of his schemes. The first Dreadnought was launched on 10 February 1907. Five days later the first three armoured

John Arbuthnot 'Jackie' Fisher in 1892, Admiral Superintendent at Portsmouth Dockyard 1891-92, Third Sea Lord and Controller, 1892-97.

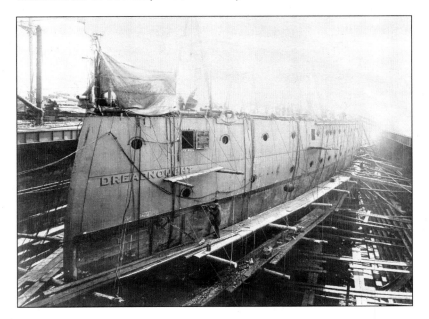

Construction of HMS Dreadnought, *1906.*

cruisers – *Invincible, Indomitable, Inflexible* – were laid down at Clydebank dockyard. The press loved it. Britain was ahead of the game. Public response was enthusiastic and some estimates noted up to 60,000 people attending Dreadnought-class launches. Commercial concerns saw a marketing opportunity, and W.D. Wills launched a range of Dreadnought cigarette cards. Fisher's motto was 'Fear God and Dread Nought'.

Despite his achievements Fisher was not popular with everyone. Opposition to his progress coalesced around the commander-in-chief of the Channel Fleet, Lord Charles ('Charlie B') Beresford. Although he had been a reformer himself in the 1880s, Beresford, who came from the Irish gentry, was the embodiment of conservative, old wardroom values. Class animosity entered into the feud and the Beresford camp liked to paint Fisher as a bourgeois upstart. The faction fighting became so public, and so disabling to the Navy, that in 1910 Fisher was obliged to resign. Beresford too was placed on the retired list.

The Spithead Fleet Review of July 1914 turned out to be a test mobilisation with 24 Dreadnoughts, 35 battleships, 49 cruisers, 76 submarines and 78 destroyers together with 100,000 'bluejackets' needed to man them.

When war was declared an efficient call-up system swung into action and reservists flooded into Portsmouth. Billeting was introduced as reservists replaced holidaymakers and the tailors and naval outfitters, Gieves and Hawkes, worked around the clock to turn out the naval uniforms required. As an echo of the Tudor's 'mightie chaine of yron' a boom defence was laid across the harbour mouth. Bravado seemed to drown out any non-combatant sentiment; when Portsmouth Labour councillor J. Mactavish attempted to speak at an anti-war meeting in the Town Hall Square on the day of the declaration, he was heckled, jeered and manhandled. An *Evening News* headline merely stated, 'Ready'. But the public, like the

HMS Dreadnought *in harbour, 1906.*

generals were, to adapt Barbara Tuchman, 'ready for the last war'. Few were prepared for what was to follow: not for the duration, nor for the proliferation of iron coffins under the North sea and South Atlantic, not for the traumatic harvesting of a generation by the military machine. By the Armistice in 1918, 1,611,000 British and Dominion soldiers had been killed and many more were recorded missing.

Xenophobia was rife, just being foreign could make you a target. A Russian-owned shop was attacked in Portsmouth despite the fact that Russia was an ally. Residents of foreign origin were made to report to local police stations for registration and finger printing. Some found themselves interned aboard ships such as the SS *Scotia* in Portsmouth Harbour. Portsmouth MP Admiral Lord Charles Beresford wrote to Prime Minister Asquith, however, querying the opportunity that these floating jailbirds got 'to have a full view of proceedings in Portsmouth Dockyard and Harbour'. A reassuring reply came from the First Lord of the Admiralty Winston Churchill indicating that precautions taken meant 'the amount of information that can be acquired by observation is not likely to be of any value'. Beresford, incidentally, through his opposition to Fisher's Edwardian-era navy reforms, had probably done more himself to undermine naval capability than these potential saboteurs!

The rate of volunteering for military service was steady but not enough. As well as government poster campaigns various other direct methods were used. Even the clergy and music-hall artistes got in on the act. In Portsmouth the Revd Bruce Cornford, vice-chairman of Portsmouth

HMS Dreadnought *in Portsmouth Harbour, c. 1906.*

Machine-gunner in stone – war memorial, Guildhall Square.

Football Club, set up a recruitment wagon at the Goldsmith Avenue end of Frogmore Road to catch Pompey fans leaving matches at Fratton Park. The appearance of a sergeant major onstage at the Kings Theatre might have been counter-productive, so music hall artistes were encouraged to include patriotic material in their acts. Vesta Tilley, for example, included a song in her Portsmouth Hippodrome performances with the verse:

Boys, take my tip and join the Army right away,
The money's good – not much, but good! – who knows
Perhaps you'll be a general some day.

The reality was that most would become a casualty statistic. The 1st Portsmouth Battalion, '11,000 men of Pompey's Own' was used by British Commander General Sir Douglas Haig in a 'diversionary operation' on the Somme. On the first day of the battle, the most disastrous in the history of the British Army, the casualty total for the whole British force was 60,000. Haig persisted with his campaign long after any strategic justification had ceased, and after twenty weeks half a million men had died. Losses at sea mirrored those on land; on the second day of the war the light cruiser *Amphion* hit a mine laid the night before in the Thames Estuary and sank with the loss of 131 lives. In the second month of the war, a U-boat sank three Royal Navy warships in one action and 1,459 sailors went down with their ships. In November 1914 at the battle of Coronel off the Chilean coast the Portsmouth-based ship HMS *Good Hope* was sunk by the heavy cruiser *Scharnhorst* and the entire complement of 900 men was lost. The uniformed telegram boy was an unwelcome presence in the city's streets; the grim news he brought was a message in a yellow envelope that read: 'Deeply regret to inform you —— was killed in action'. The statistics can come to seem like military accountancy and say nothing about the personal tragedy. James Callaghan (future Prime Minister) recalled going with his mother as a small child to visit the widow of a Copnor neighbour killed in the *Good Hope*. 'I was conscious of the grief in that room. What engraved the visit indelibly on my memory was the sight of the young widow suckling her baby at her breast.'

One set-piece naval engagement was a personal loss to many Portsmouth families. The Grand Fleet under Admiral Jellicoe and the German High Seas Fleet under Vice-Admiral Reinhard Scheer met at the end of May 1916 in the North Sea west of the Jutland peninsula. This battle produced none of the decisiveness of the battles the Nile or Trafalgar had done and, given the comparatively greater loss of life and tonnage, appeared at first to have been a British defeat, as indeed it was interpreted by the press. Jellicoe, in his Portsmouth-built dreadnought *Iron Duke*, was criticised for not prosecuting the battle vigorously enough when he had the advantage, but as Churchill pointed out, he was the only man on either side 'who could have lost the war in an afternoon'. The strategic outcome was to keep the German fleet virtually bottled up in its ports for the rest of the war. The aftermath of the battle saw 6,097 yellow-enveloped telegrams delivered to British homes, many of them in Portsmouth.

During the war the Portsmouth area was both a transit camp and a reception centre. Estimates suggest that between 25,000 and 50,000 troops were stationed there at any one time during the war years, either in encampments on Portsdown Hill or in barracks. These troops would be taken by train to Southampton to board troopships bound for France and their ships could pass other ships returning from France with the wounded. Portsmouth citizens got used to seeing columns of de-trained wounded. At first these were almost celebratory events ('returning heroes') but as the war went on, authorities became concerned about the effect endless convoys of shattered men would have on public morale. The casualties were taken to the Alexandra Military Hospital on Portsdown Hill, the infirmary at Milton (now St Mary's), the expanded Royal Navy Hospital at Haslar and a girls' school in Fawcett Road, converted into a military hospital. The first German to die of his wounds at this hospital had been buried with full military honours at Highland Road cemetery but as the numbers of dead mounted, most ceremonial was dispensed with. Some private residences, such as the Brickwoods' family house, Brankesmere in Queen's Crescent, were given over for use as military nursing homes. The shell-shocked went to the Borough Lunatic Asylum in Milton (later St James's Hospital).

Portsmouth's huge turnover of military personnel during the war produced its own social problems. A clinic for the treatment of venereal diseases was set up at Royal Portsmouth Hospital in 1917 and treated 20,000 cases in two years. At the outbreak of the war there were almost 1,000 licensed premises in Gosport and Portsmouth where drink could be bought. War shortages affected the brewing industry but nonetheless drunkenness was perceived as a threat to the war effort. More restrictive licensing orders were introduced under the Defence of the Realm Act (DORA) to eliminate 'drink-related slacking' among munitions and dockyard workers. This act was the genesis of the country's esoteric licensing restrictions which stayed in place for the rest of the century.

Codes of moral behaviour are stretched and tested under the pressure of war and guardians of public morality mounted 'women's purity patrols' in the more licentious of Portsmouth's streets. The YMCA (Young Men's Christian Association) set up a hut at Hilsea Barracks to offer 'Tommies' more wholesome leisure pursuits. Dame Aggie Weston, Christian activist and founder of the journal *Ashore and Afloat*, was the moving force behind the setting up of the Royal Sailors' Rest Home in Commercial Road. Portsmouth's Hippodrome showcased an entertainment entitled *Damaged Goods*, a morality tale about fallen women.

In Portsmouth the war also brought hardship for many women but also new job opportunities. Before 1914, over 11 per cent of Portsmouth's population had been involved in corset and stay making. With the outbreak of war, contraction in demand for the corset industry led to layoffs and short-time working. Many employers also dispensed with the services of their domestic servants and this too meant hardship for many. In these pre-Welfare State days, the response was to mobilise charity workers, hence the setting up of the National Relief Fund and the

Women workers for the Portsea Gas Light Company after completing their final shift at the end of the First World War. (Courtesy of British Gas)

Boot Fund for poor children and soup kitchens. The response was often inadequate and also demeaning for the recipients. Manpower shortages, particularly after conscription was introduced through the Military Services Act of 1916, created many new jobs for women. Women found work for the first time in a variety of new settings: the Dockyard, in the naval Ordnance Depot at Priddy's Hard filling cartridges and shells, making mines and depth charges and bagging TNT, as 'lady clerks' in the male preserve of banking, as grocery van drivers, postal delivery workers, tram conductresses and drivers, aviation workers and as Hampshire Land Army volunteers. Towards the end of the war, the Women's Royal Naval Service (WRNS) was started with the opening of an office in Lion Terrace in February 1918. Duties were mostly confined to signals, making mine nets and the maintenance of ordnance. It was another seventy-five years before Wrens were allowed to serve on warships.

Although public warning posters about aircraft identification were a familiar sight on the streets there was no mistaking the outline of a Zeppelin. In the only air raid of the war on Portsmouth, Zeppelin L31 appeared over the city at ten minutes to midnight on the 25 September 1916. It had taken off from its base at Ahlhorn on the north German coast earlier that evening and its commander only decided over

Dungeness to raid Portsmouth rather then London. Moving down the Channel and passing over Beachy Head then Selsey Bill, it described an arc over eastern Wight, Sandown and Ryde, and came in over the Point at 11,000ft to jettison its sixty bombs. Fortunately they fell harmlessly into the harbour and the Zeppelin veered east over Midhurst and returned home. Exactly six days later the same airship was strafed by a biplane over Hertfordshire and was destroyed with all her crew. The Zeppelin forays stopped but L31's night raid over Portsmouth was a searchlight prelude to a more ruthless air war that would target its citizens in a future conflict.

Less dramatic, but more deadly, were the German mine-laying tactics and the deployment of the U-boats. In the last two years of the war over fifty large merchant ships were sunk by mine or torpedo within thirty miles of the Isle of Wight. The convoy system and the Nab Tower represent a belated recognition of how vulnerable the island's supply lines were.

Widows and orphans in Portsmouth, as elsewhere, tended to be anonymous while the dead were written in stone. Thirty thousand people attended the unveiling of the Guildhall Square war memorial built to commemorate the (estimated) 6,000 men and women of Portsmouth who had been killed. The machine gunners that flank the entrance to the memorial's stone corral were made by sculptor Charles Sargeant Jagger (1885-1934), twice-wounded survivor of Gallipoli and the Western Front, who understood what he was putting into stone. The Naval War Memorial on the seafront, unveiled a year later in October 1922, is to the memory of 'those who have no other grave than the sea'.

The Nab Tower stands as the Great War's contribution to a local tradition of military follies. This 160ft steel and concrete tower was designed to be part of a projected 20-mile anti-submarine net that was to straddle the English Channel. Only two towers had been built by the war's end and this one was sunk off the coast of the Isle of Wight in 1920 to act as a lighthouse.

One day in July 1921 Field Marshal Earl Haig went to Gosport to lay the foundation stone for the Gosport War Memorial Hospital. Haig spent his remaining ten years after the war working for ex-servicemen through the Haig Fund and the Poppy Day appeal. Yet his war record as a commander who was profligate with men's lives can only cloud that day with grim irony.

CHAPTER 7

Depot

The Carnegie Library in Fratton Road opened in September 1906, eleven months after work on the site started. It had been made possible through a grant from the Foundation set up by Andrew Carnegie (1835-1919), the son of an emigrant Scottish linen weaver, who in twenty-five years had made himself owner of the largest steel works in America. When he sold that to J.P. Morgan in 1901 he became the richest man in the world. In *The Gospel of Wealth*, Carnegie had outlined an astounding philosophy – the rich were morally obliged to use their money to help those less fortunate. So in a campaign of cultural philanthropy he funded 1,679 free libraries in America and 660 in Britain between 1886 and 1917.

For the Fratton library the Council provided the land and local architects Rake and Cogswell their design services for nothing. The brief called for a main library hall with book stacks, a newspaper room, magazine room and a ladies' reading room. Initially the loan system was on a closed access basis with the readers choosing from a catalogue, checking a board for book availability and putting their request to a librarian. The library was able to move from this index system in 1920 to become the first Portsmouth library with open access to the book stacks. Carnegie libraries were the first to make serious provision for children as readers. Upstairs at the Fratton library the brief had provided for a lecture room where adult education classes could be held and Carnegie's local libraries were to become the accessible street corner universities of their day. His parallel fund to promote international peace was sadly less effective.

During the morning of 10 September 1908 HMS *St Vincent*, the latest Dreadnought, was launched from No. 5 Slip at Portsmouth Dockyard. That afternoon less than a mile away the city's mayor Ferdinand Foster with his five-year-old daughter Doris, the Education Committee and guests, led a procession from the town hall to open the new Municipal College. The *St Vincent* was the eighth warship in the Dreadnought class; it was also the fastest so far (21 knots) and the largest (19,250 tons). After the Great War she was broken up at Dover after being discarded under the terms of the 1921 Washington Treaty, an arms limitation treaty brokered by the US to try and forestall a new naval arms race. In the year 2000 the former Municipal College Building (now the Park Building) had an extensive refit and became home for the School of Language and Area Studies in the expanding University of Portsmouth.

Although newspapers like *The Times* devoted many column inches to the latest Dreadnought launches press interest in the College inaugural had been, perhaps understandably, more muted. Yet it was this event that provided further evidence that Portsmouth was maturing beyond its company town status. In the early 1890s the municipal gaze had focused on provision for the teaching of higher education in Portsmouth and in 1895 a Technical Institute was opened in disused municipal offices in Arundel Street. Institute courses on offer included Naval Architecture, Machine and Building Construction, Nautical Astronomy as well as Physiology and Hygiene. The success of this venture and the expansion of adult education generally led to a decision to consolidate teaching under one purpose-built roof.

A design competition for the new Municipal College and incorporated public library was announced in 1900, with the site designated as the triangular 'Mayor's Lawn' behind the town hall. Entrants included local architects G.E. Smith and A.E. Cogswell, with Smith emerging as the winner. This was his biggest architectural commission and it was to test his patience. Municipal delays in appointment of surveyors, organising finance and tendering for builders took the construction start date to November 1903. Changes to the brief ran in parallel to the building work. A complex heating and ventilation system and extra gas and electricity provision for laboratories pushed costs up. The building was complete in 1908 but the costs had doubled to £90,000.

The finished building housed state-of-the-art facilities: drawing offices, workshops, lecture theatres, design rooms and metallurgical and mechanical laboratories. Given its site the institute strove to establish itself tucked away behind the town hall but the rusticated Portland stone façades established a strong presence and the 140ft tower emphasized the grandeur of the entrance. Just inside the main door mosaic roundels set into the floor depicting the *Victory* and a Dreadnought were reminders of just what the city had been about. Portsmouth had lavished money on a Municipal College and a Free Library to be proud of.

On 10 February 1910, the Commander in Chief of the British Channel Fleet welcomed the Emperor of Abyssinia and his entourage for a tour of inspection of HMS *Dreadnought* at Weymouth. Advanced warning from the Foreign Office had only come three hours before. Still a marine honour guard was assembled and as the band was not familiar with Abyssinia's national anthem, they played Zanzibar's – the next best thing, perhaps. The escorting officer, through an interpreter, showed the visitors the ship's gunnery and communications assets, modestly declining the proffered Order of Abyssinia at the tour's end. No Dreadnought orders were forthcoming though from the Horn of Africa as the visit was revealed to be a hoax by pacifists and had included artist Duncan Grant and a bearded Virginia Woolf! A display of deference to royalty, coupled, perhaps, with a too keen desire to sell military hardware had apparently taken precedence over Naval security.

Portsmouth has also been connected with non-military expeditions. In the Dockyard there is a statue of Captain Robert Falcon Scott (1868-1912), explorer of Antarctica and national hero. Although his expedition to be the first to reach the South Pole failed he remains an appealing hero. It was perhaps the manner of Scott's dying that acquired heroic status with contemporaries and since – an English officer far from home and up against it.

In August 1914, just as the Great War was starting, Ernest Shackleton (1874-1922) set off in the *Endurance,* intending to cross the continent of Antarctica via the South Pole. One of the ship's company was expedition artist, George Marston, who, from an artisan background in Portsmouth, had been one of the first to take advantage of the opportunity and train as an art teacher at Regent Street Polytechnic.

William Wyllie (1851-1931) was an artist who believed in working for the common good. When Wyllie moved to Portsmouth in 1906 as an established marine artist and set up home and studio in what was to become Tower House on Portsmouth Point. Over twenty-five years he captured in his paintings all aspects of maritime life and naval history in

Sightseers are rowed out to view the SS Duchess of Kent *beached after a collision in the harbour in 1909.*

Statue of Captain Robert Scott (1868-1912), Antarctic explorer, College Road, HM Dockyard.

etching, drypoint and watercolour. He founded the first troop of the city's Sea Scouts, was one of the principal founders of Portsmouth Sailing Club, and was one of the movers who set up the Society for Nautical Research in 1910. This society played an important part in the founding of the National Maritime Museum, the Victory Museum and the rescue and restoration of HMS *Victory* itself. *Victory* had arrived back at Portsmouth in December 1812 and was paid off from active service. After two years under repair, she spent the next 100 years afloat in Portsmouth Harbour as flagship to a range of senior admirals. Steady deterioration was a consequence and in 1903 it was rammed and holed by the iron battleship *Neptune* being towed to a breaker's yard. The SNR (Society for Nautical

A view of the Point from the Round Tower. Tower House was the home of painter William Wyllie. The white-painted, clapboard Quebec House was originally a sea bathing house in 1754.

The stern of HMS Victory, berthed in No. 2 Dry Dock since 1922. She was built between 1759 and 1765 at Chatham.

Research) was instrumental in persuading the Navy to set aside No. 2 dry dock and move *Victory* there, but not until 1922. After six years of restoration work, in part funded by public donation, the ship was finally opened to visitors during the Navy Days of 1928.

There were essentially two decades of economic slump after the war with a fall in international demand for textiles, coal, iron, steel and shipbuilding and a subsequent rise in unemployment. There were 3 million unemployed in Britain during the winter of 1932-33 and 9,000 in Portsmouth in 1931. Fascism was established in Germany and Italy, and in Britain a warship modernisation programme started in 1933, accelerating towards the end of the decade. The war threat dividend for Portsmouth was at work again.

The local economy during the 1930s needed to diversify because the Navy could not be relied upon as a regular customer and the specialised skills needed in the Dockyard were not readily transferable to other enterprises. Many industries outside the defence sector were under capitalised and companies were prone to the ever-present threats of merger or take-over. The local brewing industry illustrates this. In 1900 there were fifteen brewers but by 1950 these had been reduced to three; Brickwoods, Portsmouth United and Youngs. Brickwoods had enough capacity in 1934 to make a success of shipping bottled beer to America when Prohibition ended.

Between the wars the city's suburban development northwards and eastwards attracted new pub building too. By the end of the thirties, the new pubs were plain brick roadhouses such as the Baffin's Inn (1937) and the Good Companion (1938) on the Eastern Road. These were not classic city pubs but rather designed to cater for families and possibly also the growing number of motorists. Getting about for most still meant on foot, or by bike. Portsmouth Corporation Tramways, introduced in 1901, were replaced by trolleybuses in 1936.

In the retail sector, the 1920s and '30s saw the development of the multiple and the department store. The first category included Woolworths and Timothy Whites. The latter traced the classic path of change from single local shop, an oil and dry-saltery business started in Portsea in 1848, to become a familiar high street chain of chemists and hardware stores. Over 500 branches existed nationwide in the mid-1930s.

This was perhaps the heyday of the provincial department store. Portsmouth stores included Landport Drapery Bazaar, Handleys, centrepiece of the Southsea scene, Knight and Lee, and Morants in Palmerston Road. Handleys boasted rest and writing rooms, a beauty spa and a golf school; Morants, a café lounge. The Portsea Island Mutual Co-operative Society ran its own department store in Fratton (rebuilt after a fire in 1934) and managed local food retail shops which were often the

An omnibus that once ran the Fratton to Dockyard route, bearing the distinctive Portsmouth Corporation livery (City of Portsmouth Preserved Transport Depot).

pioneer stores on new housing developments that were extending across the island east and north. Typical of the latter were the Bransbury Park estate, built by the Council with houses set in generous garden plots, and the Highbury Estate at Cosham, a development of classic 1930s semi-detached houses, and the Wymering 'Garden City'.

The city had mixed success planning for the traveller and for the tourist. In 1932 it opened an airport on land bought in the north east of the island and flights operated between here and London, the Isle of Wight, the Channel Islands and south coast towns. But an airfield with grass runways on a small site was going to find expansion difficult as commercial air travel moved from the era of the de Havilland Dragon to that of the Boeing Stratocruiser in the post-war years. One character associated with the airport story was Nevil Shute Norway (1899-1960). An aeronautical engineer who helped develop the retractable undercarriage, he was founder of the company Airspeed and was later better known as Nevil Shute, the novelist. Best-known for two novels that were made into films, *A Town Like Alice* and *On the Beach*, but he also wrote *Landfall*, set in Portsmouth, and *Requiem for a Wren*.

Most visitors and holidaymakers between the wars came by rail and, increasingly, in coaches as day-trippers. The railway lines to London were electrified in 1938. The Corporation had a long history of trying to improve the cityscape. As far back as 1891 a Parks and Open Spaces committee was set up to carry out a policy of putting bought private land to recreational use. Alexandra Park was opened in 1907 and Milton and Bransbury parks created after 1911. In 1926 it purchased Great Salterns estate provided land for a 126-acre Corporation golf course. In the 1920s the City pursued grant-aided workfare schemes such as the sea front promenade extension and the creation of the Eastern Road. In 1922 it had bought Southsea Common from the War Office; so Southsea's recreational green belt came out of the earlier need to preserve fields of fire for the services. These were fashioned into rock gardens, a fountain, a children's paddling pool and the tree-lined walkway of Ladies' Mile (1924).

The trick then, as now, was to try to extend the visitor season as far as it would go. Annual events such as Navy Week and Cowes Week became institutions. Other one-off events were imported, such as the Schneider Trophy races of 1923, 1929 and 1931. These were contests of seaplanes over a course that traced a rectangle of sky with the planes starting north of Cowes, flying east over Horse Sand Fort to Selsey and returning to the start boat close in to the South Parade shore. The seafront was the perfect viewing platform.

Sport was also a draw. Portsmouth Football Club was on the up, climbing from Third to First Division in the 1920s and appearing in three

The Uropa Club, formerly the Palace Continental Cinema built in 1924.

FA Cup finals – winning at last in 1939. Alexandra Park hosted cycle racing and athletics meetings and the nearby stadium at Tipner, opened in 1932, featuring speedway and greyhound racing. The dogs had come to Britain in 1926 as an import from the America of the roaring '20s; the tin hare was busiest in Portsmouth in the immediate post-war years.

The dramatic arts flourished; West End shows were tried out at the Kings and the Theatre Royal, the Hippodrome, the Coliseum and, at the South Parade Pier's Pavilion, was showcased variety, light opera and revue. The silver screen was located in over thirty city venues, from the north-west frontier motifs of Cogwell's designs for The Palace to the

Tivoli in Copnor Road, the Troxy Super cinema and the new Odeons in London and Festing Roads (1936 and 1937).

At the northern end of the island, the Corporation worked to bring the former Hilsea Lines back into use as a civic amenity. Rampart became gardens and the moat a water feature. As part of this civilising of the defences, the City created that essential site of 1930s leisure – the lido. Designed by the City architect, Hilsea Lido opened in 1936 and brought something of the glamour of the Italian Riviera to municipal bathing. Here was the chance for sociable group leisure in a moderne setting, for Lidos were perfect places for the streamlined machine-image architecture pursued by '30s modernists. The decks provided were natural habitats for the contemporary cultists of sun worship. The water was filtered sea-water, sterilized by ammonia and chlorine and aerated by cascades at each end of the pool. An audience of 1,000 spectators seated in deckchairs could watch the performances from the diving tower's 10-metre board.

The Corporation continued to improve amenities and market Portsmouth as a resort. It started an inspection and listing scheme for guesthouses and hotels and it provided sea-front kiosks, shelters, sun huts and deck chairs. In 1930 it issued 32,000 guidebooks to inquirers. The tone and register of these guides make them interesting records of some contemporary attitudes. The City of Portsmouth and Southsea *Coronation Year Guide* of 1937 makes much of that year's Coronation Fleet Review. This Coronation had been occasioned by the abdication of Edward VIII who had plans to marry a divorcee, then a taboo in the culture of royalty. In the early hours of the morning of 12 December 1936, Edward was driven by car into Portsmouth Dockyard to board HMS *Fury*. The aircraft carrier and its escort HMS *Bloodhound* took the ex-king into exile in France. King George was welcomed in a loyal preface to the City's 1937 Guide on the occasion that 'HM the King comes to review His Navy in the waters of Spithead, the waters that guard our inheritance. God Save the King!' The writer describes the *Victory*, for instance as a sort of 'ethnic touchstone: she is a shrine. When man or boy sets foot on Nelson's ship, he cannot be of British race, unless some strange emotion stirs him.' More prosaically he adds that the Royal Marine guides on the ship explain 'every tiny detail, amplifying their discourse with amusing anecdotes.'

Another guide produced by Carter and Lancaster, estate agents, was intended for potential house-buyers. Given that the concept of the commuter hadn't been properly patented yet, these buyers could have included the London businessman who might want to 'make his home by the sea' – the London to Southsea rail journey took 90 minutes. Clearly these guides needed to put a positive gloss on present lives but two items in the City's 1937 Guide inadvertently signalled some facets of approaching conflict and change. The one shilling entrance charge to

Marines in a parade at HMS St Vincent, *Gosport, in 1938. This sort of display is typical of parades seen in Portsmouth and Gosport over the years.*

SILVER JUBILEE ILLUMINATIONS OF THE FLEET AT SPITHEAD. JULY. 1935

JOHN ABRAHAMS.
Naval and Press Photographer
9 QUEEN STREET. PORTSMOUTH

A postcard commemorating the Fleet Review of 1935, on the occasion of George V's Silver Jubilee.

all the Navy Week attractions allowed the visitor access to an L-class submarine. Portsmouth's airport, with its great hangars, refreshment chalets, garages and wireless control stations, was offered as the shape of things to come. Langstone Harbour, nearby, would eventually 'become the greatest Empire flying boat base in the world'. It would take a little over a decade to show this to have been optimism rather than a prediction. The Langstone scheme flying boats would become history and the Empire would follow and submarines would make an impact sooner than that.

Nevil Shute spent part of 1938 sitting at home in 14 St Helena Road, Southsea writing his novel, *What Happened to the Corbetts*, 'to show what air raids really would be like'. Set in Southampton the book portrays a city having its infrastructure torn apart; gas, water and sewage mains burst, craters in roads and the awful blasts of bombs. In an epilogue addressed to the citizens of Southampton, Shute explained his purpose; to jog officials into precautionary action and raise the general level of awareness about the terrible things all city dwellers 'may one day have to face together'. After the fall of France in 1940 that day came for Portsmouth.

As for preparations, there wasn't much to go on. The air-raid atrocity at Guernica in 1937, where the Junkers and Heinkels of the German Condor Legion destroyed this ancient Basque town in an afternoon, was carried out against an undefended target and without warning. Before war was declared on Sunday 3 September 1939, plans for the evacuation of Portsmouth's children had swung into action and 12,000 had left the city for Salisbury, the Isle of Wight and Hampshire villages and towns. Sandbags appeared around street shelters and blackout restrictions were enforced with the threat of a prison sentence. One immediate result was a rise in fatal road accidents as vehicles with masked headlights toured unlit streets. Increasingly the civilian population was enlisted into the war effort and by October 1940, civilian labour had constructed 2,200 brick shelters, communal shelters for 5,000, and 24,000 Anderson shelters. There were over a thousand full-time ARP wardens.

The Blitz air offensive against British urban targets gathered momentum in August and September 1940 with the largest raids launched against London. From the first air attack on Portsmouth in July 1940 until the end of May 1944, the city sustained sixty-seven air raids. In total 930 civilians were killed in these raids and a further 1,216 were injured badly enough to need hospitalisation. As a prime naval base and dockyard it was always going to be a target; it was 60 miles from France and its coastal position made it easy to locate.

The night raid of 10 January 1941 was one of the heaviest on Portsmouth during the war. German planes from Luftflotte III formed up from air bases across the Low Countries and France. 300 Heinkel 111s came in above the barrage balloons and over fire from anti-aircraft batteries at Sinah Common, Gilkicker and Southsea Common, through carbon arc-light beams of searchlights to drop 350 tons of high explosive on the city. The result was 171 dead, 430 injured and 3,000 homeless. People emerged to find parts of the city missing or altered. The shopping centres of Commercial Road, Kings Road and Palmerston Road had been hit hard with Landport Drapery Bazaar, Knight and Lee and Handleys ablaze. Woolworths, the Royal Sailors Rest and the Co-operative Department store in Fratton Road had been destroyed, along with the George Hotel in Old Portsmouth, Clarence Pier, six churches, the Connaught Drill Hall, part of the Royal Hospital, the Hippodrome, the Dockyard School, the Central Hotel and three cinemas. Cinemas seemed to be ill-fated; during a raid the month before, a bomb had exploded in the projectionist's room of the Carlton Cinema in Cosham High Street, killing fifty people. In the January raid the greatest symbolic loss for the city was caused by two incendiary bombs that entered one of the Guildhall's ventilator shafts. Burst water mains had meant the resulting fire was left to burn for twelve hours reducing the building to a gutted shell. Winston Churchill visited the city on 31 January and as he toured the ruined streets was met with cheering and clapping citizens.

Portsmouth and its citizens were truly in the front line for the first time since the fourteenth century. Citizens were exhorted by billboards to 'Dig for Victory', 'Keep Mum', 'Let Hitler Feel Pompey's Punch' (a slogan for the War Weapons Week fund-raising drive), 'Is Your Journey Really

Detail from the Second World War part of the Royal Naval Memorial on Southsea Common.

Necessary?' and 'Women of Britain Come into the Factories'. Women from the Hampshire Company of the ATS worked as drivers and dispatch riders out of the Motor Transport Depot and manned the anti-aircraft batteries, as 'ack-ack girls'; they worked as barrage balloon crews in the Women's Auxiliary Air Force, at the Southern Railways workshops at Eastleigh, as ARP wardens and as assault boat construction workers at the Wooton Yard.

Portsmouth provided the first women drivers of double-decker buses and the Wrens were given a larger role in this war, including the servicing of fighter planes at the RN Air Station at Lee-on-Solent. British Restaurants, such as the one in Albert Road, offered a subsidized three-course lunch for 10d; childcare facilities were provided. War seemed to have made most things possible.

A grimmer aspect, that recalled the experiences of the Great War, was the effect on the city of the losses at sea. Unlike the protracted wait for the start of the war in the air, the war at sea began on Day 1. On 3 September U-boat U-30 torpedoed the liner *Athenia* outbound from Liverpool. The sinking of this vessel with the loss of 112 lives signalled the start of the Battle of the Atlantic, arguably the most important theatre of operations for Britain in the whole war. Men from Portsmouth played their part in the crews of Corvettes and other warships which tried to protect merchant convoys from U-boat attack, often in appalling conditions. U-boat lone raiders and wolfpacks sank 2,828 merchant ships during the war and almost succeeded in starving Britain into surrender. The allocation of enough aircraft to cover the surface escorts in May 1943 prevented this disaster.

It was a similar miscalculation about the need for aircraft in the war at sea that accounted for some of the losses of the Royal Navy's capital ships, that and the vulnerability of those ships to U-boats and to the new type of German battleship (built in defiance of the arms limitation treaty). On the third Sunday of the war, a U-boat sank the aircraft carrier *Courageous* in the Bristol Channel. The next day U-47 penetrated the Navy's main Home Waters anchorage at Scapa Flow and torpedoed the battleship *Royal Oak*. The Navy had been convinced that sonar would neutralise the U-boat threat. The situation was made worse by the sinking of the carrier *Glorious* by the pocket battleships *Scharnhorst* and *Gneisenau* in June 1940 as she returned from the campaign in Norway.

Further spectacular reverses involved the sinking of battleships *Repulse* and *Prince of Wales* by Japanese torpedo-bombers in December 1941. There had been naval successes: at Taranto against the Italian navy; the hounding to destruction of the pocket battleship *Graf Spee* and the ultimately successful hunt for the battleship *Bismarck*. Yet to so many Portsmouth homes the postman brought that dreaded official letter of condolence. Perhaps most symbolic was the sinking in May 1941 of the battle cruiser HMS *Hood* – obliterated by a salvo from the *Bismarck* and taking down with her over 1,400 men. HMS *Hood*, a Portsmouth Navy Days attraction only six years before, was a link with the era of the Grand Fleet and an emblem of that old confidence in battleships and British naval superiority.

In August 1942 the 2nd Canadian Infantry Division made a frontal assault on the port of Dieppe. The force sailed from Portsmouth to carry out a dummy run raid before the real assault on occupied Europe. The attack was not backed up by sufficient naval or air support and was a failure with large Canadian losses. The concept of the raid was much criticised but demonstrated the difficulty there would be in capturing a French port intact such that it might act as a supply route for invading forces. The new plan was to build and transport a floating breakwater: a Mulberry Harbour. In a feat reminiscent of the heroics of Victorian engineering, 45,000 men worked to build the 212 concrete and steel caissons required, at sites from the Thames to Langstone, at Stokes Bay and Portsmouth. 132 ocean going tugs would tow the caissons across to the Normandy coast. In Portsmouth Dockyard and at Vospers yard workers created the 1,000 landing craft needed for the assault on the Normandy beaches.

As D-Day approached, Portsmouth and its coastal hinterland became a vast depot and an exclusion zone. Accommodation needed to be found in the city for the 29,000 personnel working on projects for D-Day; church halls, boarding houses, hotels, schools and cinemas were requisitioned. Behind Portsdown Hill armies were gathered, bivouacked in the woods of south Hampshire with columns of armoured vehicles tailing back along

Sherman tank outside the D-Day Museum. These workhorses of the Allied tank divisions were dubbed 'Ronsons' as they were quick to catch fire when hit.

arterial roads. Inside the Hill beneath Fort Southwick the Combined Operations plotting and coding rooms became the nerve centre of Operations Overlord and Neptune. In the harbours and anchorage below, the craft were so densely packed that, it was said, you could practically walk across to the Isle of Wight from deck to deck. In a trailer close to Southwick House, General Eisenhower, Overlord's supreme commander, worried about getting the day right. When it was 'Go', some of the embarking troops walked out on a scaffolded walkway connected to South Parade Pier, bound for France.

At the war's end, many of the public made much of the VE Day bonfires and parties and crowds gathered in the Guildhall Square to listen to the King's speech. Yet the service personnel's response was often just one of relief that it was all over. One naval officer returning with his ship from Malta recalled: 'The war was over for me. There wasn't much of a hero's welcome; half a dozen wives and a handful of scruffy dockyard mateys – but who cared?'

Portsmouth had a pivotal role in the launching of the largest amphibious invasion in history and could take pride in its association with D-Day's aim – to open a second front and eliminate fascism from mainland Europe. This pride took a material form in the creation of the Overlord Embroidery, a sort of Bayeux Tapestry in reverse, designed by artist Sandra Lawrence whose sketches and water colours provided the templates for the embroidery's panels. The idea of a war artist, someone who is commissioned by the state to produce an official record of the war, goes back a long way – at least as far as Van der Velders, who was commissioned by Charles II. In the First World War artists Muirhead Bone and John Duncan Ferguson were assigned to the Grand Fleet at Rosyth and Portsmouth, respectively. Ferguson's *Dockyard, Portsmouth* (1918) focused on the warship feature of 'dazzle' – painting the ship's sides in irregular colours and shapes to confuse an enemy plotting the ship's movements. Artist to the Admiralty, Richard Eurich (1903-1992), painted Portsmouth at war and is best known for *Preparations for D-Day* and *Night Raid on Portsmouth Docks* (1941). Preparatory work for these was done from an observation tower high above the Dockyard. One war assignment took Eric Ravilious to HMS *Dolphin* in 1941 where he produced a haunting series of lithographs known as the 'Submarine Series'.

CHAPTER 8

Flagship

April 1949 at Fratton Park was a moment to savour as Pompey's captain Reg Flewin hoisted the First Division Championship cup after the club had topped the League – five points ahead of Manchester United! In the following season (1949-50) Portsmouth did it again – just – by goal average, after tying on points with Wolverhampton Wanderers. Wolves and the Busby Babes would be the dominant teams of the fifties. Sadly, Pompey was to win nothing again in the next five decades. In the local newspaper photograph of the event, standing slightly to the right of the triumphant captain, is the figure of Bernard Law Montgomery – Monty of Alamein in his trademark beret – gesturing approval, just above a row of expectant Tannoy loudspeakers and the focus of the crowd's attention. In the 1950s he was an important figure in NATO and wrote books in his retirement. By the time of his death in 1976, and with more time for reflection, more revisionist accounts of the Second World War were sometimes critical of the Field Marshal's war time role.

Football has sometimes been taken too seriously, then as today, but it can sometimes be a metaphor and reflect changes in other aspects of life: Jimmy Dickinson was the archetypal post-war one-club player. During a twenty-year involvement with Pompey, he created a club record of 834 appearances and twice played 100 consecutive league games. He was modestly paid (£10 a week in the 1950s) and 'gentlemanly' – he was never sent off. In the mercantilist atmosphere of contemporary commercial football, Jimmy Dickinson seems as dated as cigarette cards.

When particular industries or trades no longer act as signifiers of towns or cities, an urban game like football can provide some of the few facts about a place anyone beyond its boundaries will know. Equally a Fratton End chanting, 'We love you Portsmouth, we do!' provides as authentic a voice of the city today as a fourteenth-century charter or some civic ceremonial.

The post-war city needed to grow and to renew its war-torn urban fabric. In 1944 a site of about 2,000 acres had been acquired at Leigh Park, north of Havant and Portsmouth Council envisaged developing it into the 'Garden City of the South'. The immediate post-war reality saw Nissen huts co-resident with prefabricated bungalows. But from 1947 this 'satellite town' began to take shape and the first residents moved there in 1949. As a hinterland, frontier estate it was separate from, but never independent of,

The Guildhall.

the city. In the early days most Leigh Park men still worked in the Dockyard and cycled there. Shopping for the new residents came in the form of vans until Park Parade opened in 1955 – a year before a regular bus service link with Portsmouth. In the 1950s there were also schools, a pub, a football club, a library and a Young Wives Group; the 1960s brought a purpose-built community centre and a Miss Leigh Park contest.

By the 1970s the population of Leigh Park and Crookhorn was 40,000. This development was Portsmouth's version of similar post-war treks out to new towns that were appearing elsewhere around major conurbations in the country. In 1971 Portsmouth's population was almost 197,000, compared with a 1931 total of 249,000. Whatever dispersal there was to satellite towns, the island city remained the most densely populated urban area in the country.

Cities need their civic monuments. They are a source of pride and identity for the population. Portsmouth Guildhall had remained a burnt-out ruin since the firebombing raid of 10/11 January 1941 and the architect Berry Webber, designer of Southampton Civic Centre, was commissioned in 1955 to create a new Guildhall in the shell of the old. The restored Guildhall, opened in 1959. It was later to be confronted, across the parade ground-like square, by the smoked-glass, L-shaped box of the Civic Offices, centre piece of Lord Esher's 1970s redevelopment plan. One building demolished to make way for this was Verrecchia's ice cream parlour and coffee bar. Sensible curators at the city museum rescued and put on display a Verrechia's booth; they were sharp enough to know that such small, but intimate details, feature large on most people's personal maps of a city.

Portsmouth's town centre reconstruction was slow and the new Commercial Road area development achieved none of the coherence of those appearing in Southampton, Plymouth or Le Havre. Commercial Road was unfortunately to be 'New Town bland' but it had a new brash neighbour to contend with – the Tricorn Centre built by architect Owen Luder. An unusual concept in this country when it opened in 1966, this megastructure, the size of a city block, had several purposes: wholesale market, social housing provision, space for a street market, shopping centre, clubs and a pub (The Casbah) and a multi-storey car park – a kind of fort for cars. Some architects then were intrigued by the streetscapes of North African and Italian hilltop towns and sought to replace the predictable geometry of the new shopping streets with randomness and urban intimacy. But this Pompey 'souk' never caught on; recession hit and shop space and flats remained unlet; design faults resulted in rain water being thrown onto parked cars and there were sights of mothers with young children battling with the gales on exposed stair towers. The sun never reached the central square and rainwater collected on the decks. Concrete allows for wondrous sculptural shapes but is not good for adaptation; it became porous and began to spall. The wholesale market seemed to work well but the Tricorn became a target for regular criticism.

Confusion over suitable urban design was matched by confusion over urban transport. The 1963 Buchanan Report talked of traffic as a function of buildings and of the need to separate the pedestrian from the car; but planners and politicians it seems didn't address the issues. Growth in car use gives personal freedom but it degrades cities in its wake. Portsmouth as a city is compact and flat and has a cycling past. A shipwright apprentice in the 1950s recalled how, at knocking off time, thousands of cyclists would leave the Dockyard; the 'traffic was just cycles for five or ten minutes, all the traffic more or less stopped to let the dockies out.' Dedicated cycle routes have been built in Gosport and the

The Tricorn building – completed in 1966 and now due for demolition.

The Tricorn building – architecture as concrete sculpture.

Flats on the western edge of Somerstown, seen from Mercantile House, at the start of a refurbishment programme in early 2001.

University initiated a 'Bike-about' scheme but we have a long way to go before we can claim an integrated transport system in Portsmouth such as that enjoyed in a city like Freiburg where pedestrians, cyclists and trams predominate.

During the most productive time for building social housing in the twenty-five years after the war, the tower block proved the most controversial form – introducing high-rise into a low-rise culture. The architects saw only light and outlook and images of modernity; the critics saw state authoritarianism and failed social engineering. They would be on surer ground talking about untried prefabrication methods, poor services and the lack of semi-public 'defensible space'. By the 1970s new policies diverted funds into the rehabilitation of existing housing stock, through improvement grants, and so saved and improved Portsmouth's stock of affordable housing and its defining townscape of terraced houses. In Portsmouth all of the inner city blocks built in the 1960s survived and Wilmcote House in Sommerstown provided the model of block rehabilitation in the 1990s; twelve other tower blocks and redundant office blocks were undergoing a programme of colourful re-cladding at the time of writing.

A drawing by Gordon Cullen from the 1960s shows a circuit linear town of continuous and sinuous high-rise buildings – improbably hugging hills above the Solent in the manner of a Le Corbusier plan for Algiers. It was a conceptual drawing that offered the kind of urban coherence only realised on some of Britain's new university campuses. The common reality tending to be urban design more through a lack of planning accompanied by transport attrition.

In 1957 Portsmouth had nineteen cinemas but by 1987 it had only three. As elsewhere, new forms of leisure and television accounted for most of this decline; a virtually redundant British film industry was a result. Feature films themselves can provide vivid, if subjective, evidence of cultural change. In the 1950s most films portrayed the war in stories of straight but understated heroics: *The Cruel Sea* (1953) starred Jack Hawkins as a corvette commander in the battle of the Atlantic. Hawkins and the ubiquitous John Mills provided the model heroes, decent and wryly laconic under pressure. Mills was in the 1958 release *I Was Monty's Double* (confusingly shown in America as *Hell, Heaven and Hoboken*). In the 1960s some films presented military norms in a more critical way.

A redundant office block rehabilitated as housing – close to Commercial Road shopping precinct, 2001.

Billy Budd (1962), starring Terence Stamp, recounted the tale of a young seaman sentenced to be hanged for killing a sadistic master-at-arms on an eighteenth-century British warship. Joseph Losey's *King and Country* (1964) looked at the court martial and execution of a front-line private in the First World War when shell-shock was no excuse for desertion; an issue that is still contemporary.

Two 1970s films were made on location in Portsmouth, both directed by Ken Russell. *The Boy Friend*, a period pastiche about a 1920s theatrical touring company, was shot in 1971 in the then redundant Theatre Royal; previously it had been the venue for another form of pretence – the burlesque of professional wrestling! Russell's other film on location created real drama of its own; during the 1974 filming of *Tommy* on South Parade Pier, a fire gutted the Edwardian interior. In the decade and a half after the war the British holiday industry had boomed and a resort like Blackpool could attract 7 million visitors a year in the 1950s; visitors could expect to meet people from their home town and home-from-home was the watchword. In 1950s Southsea comedian, Tommy Trinder and Hammond organ concerts were packing in the crowds at South Parade Pier and large crowds, seated in ranks of deck chairs, watched bikini-clad girls parade up and down in 'Miss This' and 'Miss That' competitions. For the holiday camp operators, Warners, Butlins and Pontins, the two post-war decades were their golden era.

In the initial post-war years the airlines BEA and BOAC formed a controlling cartel but in 1950 an entrepreneur was permitted to use a converted Dakota aircraft to fly students and teachers only, to Corsica for an inclusive camping holiday. The company was Horizon and the package holiday was born. In 1949 about 200,000 people crossed the Channel annually; by 1999 over 14 million Britons a year took an overseas package holiday. The British seaside holiday as a mass experience was over.

In 1962 American Secretary of State Dean Acheson pronounced that Britain had 'lost an empire and not yet found a role.' This could also have been said of Portsmouth. The Navy was shedding its role as a global patrolman and the Dockyard was shedding labour. In 1950 the yard employed around 26,000 and currently (2001) the figure is close to 2,000. Defence thinking has moved away from reliance on a large surface fleet and in 1968 HMS *Andromeda* was the last warship to be built in the yard. In possibly the last operation of its kind a naval Task Force left Portsmouth in April 1982 to regain control of the Falkland Islands from the Argentinians. As in days of old dockers had worked round the clock to fit out the fleet but this time with redundancy notices in their pockets.

As the present role is scaled down, more of the past becomes valued and valuable as a commodity. Increased interest in industrial archaeology has helped give industrial buildings and objects more status. Even industrial

*The former officers'
block of Cambridge
Barracks (built 1898),
now the City's Museum,
Art Gallery and Record
Office.*

warehouses can take on a new lease of life; the Dockyard's Storehouse 11 (built 1763-66) has been beautifully restored and refurbished and become the centrepiece of the Royal Naval Museum. English Heritage rescued one Palmerston fort and the Royal Armouries another. One turreted block of the old Clarence Barracks was opened as the City Museum and Art Gallery. The beam engine at Eastney pumping station is now an industrial heritage site.

Amid a fanfare of national attention the *Mary Rose* was recovered from the seabed in 1982 together with a cache of artefacts entombed within

her. HMS *Warrior* was brought out of ignominy as a Milford Haven oil jetty, restored and returned to her home port of Portsmouth in 1987; these ships now offer some of the city's most evocative sights and in the case of the latter, some fascinating interior spaces. Flagship Portsmouth is now a major attraction and large numbers of visitors are seen every year: 500,000 came to the Naval base in 1999-2000. The Royal Yacht, often to be seen moored at Whale Island when operational, has become a tourist attraction.

Redundant property from Defence estates is regularly released onto the market and it has often been acquired by the growing university. So a former barracks came to house criminologists and sociologists; the United Services officer's club was remade into a chaplaincy and housed a counselling service; a NAAFI building was recycled into a students' union. The university has become a major employer, landlord and player in the local economy, as well as a more visible presence in the city, from its Langstone campus to its flagship Portland and Park buildings. It will soon lease a refurbished, redundant city-centre office block as student accommodation. In the immediate post-war period the Municipal College drew on a catchment area of neighbouring counties. It grew and changed status from College of Technology in 1953 to polytechnic in 1969 and university in 1992. The current institution has an office dedicated to the recruitment of overseas students.

Many urban councils have developed the arts and culture as a way of boosting city recognition. In spite of a burgeoning student population (currently over 15,000) Portsmouth appears to find it difficult to give the arts a high profile: annual festivals in the 1980s and 1990s (especially the Guildhall Square Big Top musical events) could not be sustained;

The First International Festival of the Sea was held in Portsmouth in 1998. The dockside canopy was erected in 1897 to shelter royal personages arriving and departing by train.

an arts centre in a suburban location struggled to make an impact and by 2000 there was no independent cinema. The Aspex gallery presents consistently innovative modern art shows but the public, it seems, has to be reminded it is there.

Independent music has thrived anyway. One post-war high was the first Isle of Wight pop festival in 1969. In August, a month after the great Woodstock festival in America, music fans were in transit through Portsmouth, a kind of musical expeditionary force, heading for the island to witness Bob Dylan and others from a giant encampment. Some, perhaps, had been kitted out at Lord Kitchener's Valet in Carnaby Street and no doubt many were feeling 'contempt for the material world'.

The Portsmouth folk scene in the 1960s thrived at venues such as the Railway Hotel and the Star, in Lake Road, booking acts from the Incredible String Band to Paul Simon. Clubs like the Birdcage featured Rod Stewart or Rick Mayall. Country Joe and the Fish played South Parade Pier. Author Anthony Rollinson has trawled his memory and sourced material from fanzines like *Dinlo*, to compile a history of this shifting phenomenon in *Twenty Missed Beats: The Portsmouth Music Scene 1977-1996*. The names of some of these Portsmouth bands testify to the shifting genres of the times: Emptifish, Polemic Attack, Sister Morphine, Periscope, Full Metal Racket, Mild-Mannered Janitors, Ad-Nauseam, etc. In 1993 the Wedgewood Rooms opened in Albert Road and provided the city with a recognised independent music venue.

In 1949 in a mutual gesture of reconciliation Portsmouth became a Partnerstadt with Duisberg – a twinning partnership. Situated in the industrial Ruhr with the Eisenwerke of Thyssen, Krupp and Mannesmann, the city had been a Bomber Command and Flying Fortress target and by the end of the war, 80 per cent of its houses had been destroyed or badly damaged. It had originated as a Hafenstadt of the Hanseatic League trading alliance and has grown to become the largest inland port in Europe with port facilities spread along 37 kilometres of the Rhine. Gerardus Mercator, cartographer and polymath, originator of the atlas and the map projection to aid navigators, was a prominent citizen there in the 1500s and the city established its first university in the mid-1600s. Today Duisberg's attractions include a Schiffahrtsmuseum, the European Centre for Modern Sculpture and Germany's first communal cinema. The arts flourish with two theatres, Deutsche Oper, a Philharmonic Orchestra and a major annual festival, the Duisberger Akzente. An urban railway network opened in 1992.

In recent years Portsmouth has succeeded in attracting foreign firms to its environs. The inscrutable smoked-glass tower bordering Victoria Park announces Zurich Insurance. The British headquarters of IBM (Arup Associates) was built on reclaimed land at North Harbour – one of

Refurbished landscape of Wilmcote House, Somerstown, built in 1967.

The Zürich Insurance building next to Victoria Park.

the first office campuses in the country. The neat Brittany Ferries office block stands some way off from the low-rent ferry port terminal building. That company's story is one to inject some excitement into a Business School seminar. In 1973 a co-operative of Breton farmers launched a ferry operation in the form of a converted landing craft shipping cauliflowers and passengers between Roscoff and Plymouth. Almost thirty years later, a multi-million pound company carries passengers and freight on luxury ferries between the English and Irish ports of Portsmouth, Plymouth and Cork and the French and Spanish ports of Caen, St Malo, Roscoff and Santander. In May 2001 the keel-laying ceremony took place in Holland for a vessel, purpose-built for the Caen-Portsmouth route. The M/V *Mont St Michel* is expected to be ready in 2002.

Joe Jackson, in his memoir about becoming a musician, *A Cure for Gravity,* recalls growing up in the Paulsgrove in the 1950s. He retains his affection for Portsmouth and wistfully recalls the taste of fish and chips, the smell of seaweed, the pubs. But he knows that nostalgia also has harder edges: in Pompey, he recalls, sailors were 'skates', and the women who came down from London by the coachload when there were a few ships in port, were called 'skate-bait.' As for the seagulls, they were known as 'shitehawks.' He also recalls that the prospect of moving from Portsmouth to Gosport was like moving from 'Manhatten to Staten Island'.

Everyone is creating heritage attractions and Gosport stole a march on its bigger neighbour by pushing on with its Millennium Promenade linking the submarine museum at Haslar to the new museum at the former armaments depot, Priddy's Hard. Across the water in the Dockyard, Boathouse 6, the handsome receiving shed for boat repairs, has been remodelled into a venue for 'interactive naval experiences',

'Action Stations' and a cinema showing 'The Navy: the Movie'. Further south HMS *Vernon*'s instruction campus for torpedo maintenance and navy divers has transmuted into Gunwharf Quays, a leisure, factory outlet and up-market housing development. The harbour's renaissance is a significant development for Portsmouth, opening up new land and seascapes to the resident and the tourist's gaze.

As the M275 curves south, through the motorway dead-zone, to cross the Tipner Lake Bridge, sculptures come into view through the motorist's windscreen, first sails, then some masts. These installations were erected early in 2001 to announce the city to the motorist, just as city gates had done to the horseman. The sculptures are of stainless steel and carry a Tri-sail 130ft high and made of French, Ferrari plastic-coated mesh. The masts are cunningly studded with blue lights and stake out a bridge that looks below onto three beached and redundant submarines and across the harbour to Portchester Castle. Perhaps they also signal a future when the aim will be to harness the waves rather than rule them.

BMX biker jumping steps at Point Battery. (Photograph by Martin Bardell)

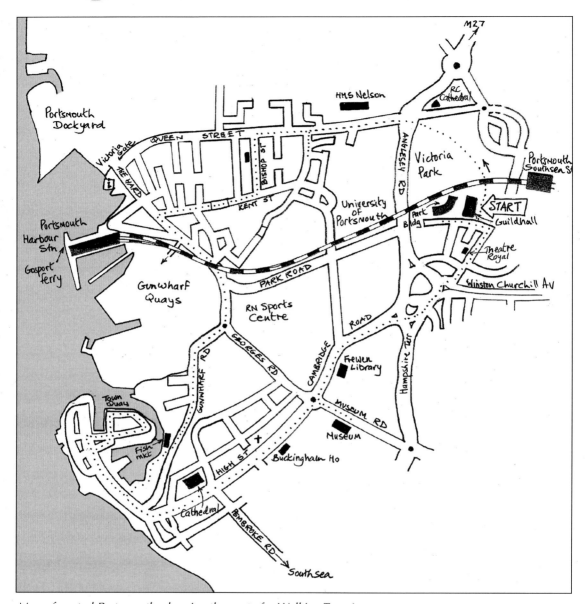

Map of central Portsmouth, showing the route for Walking Tour 1.

WALKING TOUR 1
Guildhall Square to Portsmouth Point

The walk is about 2 Qw miles long and stays largely within the town centre area so leaving it to return to car parking or public transport access at any time is simple.

Start in the Guildhall Square facing the statue of Queen Victoria.

This 9ft tall bronze incarnation of the Queen, looking suitably imperial, was made when she was in fact an empress at the head of the world's largest empire. She faces the Guildhall and diagonally to her right are the statues of two machine gunners and the city's war memorial.

Walk over to the memorial and its sculptured protectors.

This semi-circular canyon of stone sheltering an obelisk was originally dedicated in October 1921 to honour Portsmouth's sons (and three of its daughters) who fell in the Great War. The sculptures are by Charles Sargeant Jagger (1885-1934) an artist who was a veteran of the same war and a recipient of the Military Cross. He was wounded at Gallipoli and again, near-fatally, during the Western Front campaign of 1918.

HMS Warrior at permanent mooring by the Hard.

Walking Tour 1

The Seagull in Broad Street; a former Brickwoods pub, built around 1910 and probably designed by architect Vernon Inkpen.

He also designed the Royal Artillery Memorial at Hyde Park Corner in London.

> **The memorial acts as a gateway that takes you next through a tunnel under the railway embankment to Victoria Park beyond. Head across the park towards the western gate, with a lodge, keeping the Palm House on your left.**

To your right beyond the park is the red-brick Roman Catholic Cathedral of St John the Evangelist (built 1877-82). Notice a collection of monuments, some rescued from road improvement schemes, most of which salute the exploits of naval brigades in China; one to HMS *Orlando* houses a captured bell in a faux Chinese temple and another a column surmounted by a lion, erected to 'commemorate the untiring efforts of a gallant officer and true-hearted man in advancing the welfare of the British Sailor.' This was paid for by 'other ranks' to honour Admiral Sir Charles Napier (1786-1860). He is not to be confused with the soldier of the same name, Sir Charles Napier (1782-1853), whose career is remembered, among other things, for his recapture of the Indian province of Sind and his telegram which signalled his success to the authorities, 'peccavi' (Latin for 'I have sinned') – a joke for the cognoscenti!

> **Leave the park and cross at the pedestrian lights to reach the top of Queen Street.**

This is Portsea's main thoroughfare. Across the road on the right is the Royal Naval Barracks HMS *Nelson* which, though now much modernised, was originally built between 1899 and 1903.

> **Head west along Queen Street.**

Along this road you will pass on your left the 'floridly Jacobean' mass of the commissioned officers' ward room block. Its dining room features two large murals of the battles of Copenhagen and the Glorious First of June painted by William Wyllie (viewable on Heritage Open Days in early September).

> **Further down Queen Street, turn left into St James's Street.**

Walking Tour 1

Ahead of you is the white modernist façade of the Portland Building. Opened in 1996 and designed by Hampshire County architect Sir Colin Stansfield-Smith, this is the University's Faculty of the Environment. The distinctive stair towers were designed to function as solar energy collectors, or chimneys, to heat and ventilate the building. The building's full-height, glazed atrium space is worth a look – a stunning piece of interior design.

> *Retrace your steps to Queen Street and turn left. After a couple of hundred yards, turn left again into Bishop Street.*

A few paces along on the right is Treadgolds. This ironmongers shop was established in 1809 and run mostly as a family business until 1988. It is a prime example of a Victorian retail business and back-street industrial site. Open to the public now as a museum, it is a redolent reminder of Victorian commercial life and is worth a visit.

> *Continue down Bishop Street and turn right at the Portsea Arms.*

Just past the next road on your right, Curzon Howe Road, stop to have a look at the Beneficial Society School (architect William Hay, 1784). This is an unusual, surviving example of a Georgian charitable school. See the informative plaque high up on the Kent Street façade.

Continue along Kent Street and then College Street and you arrive at the Hard. The main route of this tour takes us left at this point but consider two additional options: (1) turning right will take you into the Dockyard and access to Portsmouth's historic ships, HMS *Victory*, *Warrior* and the *Mary Rose*, associated museums, naval experiences and harbour tours; (2) taking a short ferry trip across the water to Gosport to see Haslar Hospital, the Submarine Museum, Gosport Museum and Priddy's Hard. Both of these options require time to see and enjoy properly and you may choose to do them on another occasion but it is certainly worth making the return ferry trip to Gosport (about eight minutes each way) just to experience the views of the harbour. To get to the Gosport Ferry negotiate the bus station interchange and head past the Harbour station to the ferry landing stage; there are coin-operated ticket machines half way down.

(*Note there is a Tourist Information Office to the seaward side of the Dockyard gate that is a useful source of pamphlets and information about local attractions, including those in Gosport.*)

Walking Tour 1

> **Turn left out of College Street and cross the main road by the empty office block, Brunel House.**

This building signals Portsea as the birthplace of the Victorian civil engineer and genius, Isambard Kingdom Brunel (1806-59). The building is a witty counterpoint to Brunel's own exciting designs. You will now pass the entrance, through a tunnel in the railway embankment, that leads to Gunwharf Quays, Portsmouth's newest (opened 2001) retail centre, created in the redundant naval shore establishment and ordnance yard, HMS *Vernon*. From this new development there are excellent views of the harbour, so even if you don't have any shopping to do, have a look in here and then return to this point.

> **Keep walking along St George's Road and pass the tattoo parlour.**

Across the road is a row of surviving Georgian houses (Ordnance Row) and the start of St George's Square which opens out to reveal at its focal point, St George's church. Built in 1754, this square-shaped grey and red-brick church with a white cupola brings a suggestion of New England to this part of Portsea. Go under the railway bridge and walk along St George's Road, following the Gunwharf wall round into Gunwharf Road. Soon, in the middle distance, you will see the Cathedral's tower with its louvred wooden cupola, topped by a golden ball and weather vane.

Head towards the Cathedral, passing the Isle of Wight car ferry terminal on your right and passing to the right of the American bar and Flounders Restaurant. Keep the Camber Quay fish market to your right and find a chain motif set in the pavement and follow it. Skirting the Camber you will come out onto Broad Street just past the clapboard boat-house. Turn right and walk down past the ship's chandlers and take the next right to the dockside.

Explore the Camber dockside with its fishing boat fleet. The working harbour is becoming surrounded by improved and 'gentrified' housing and other developments. Look out for the gable wall of the Bridge Tavern with its mural version of Thomas Rowlanson's 'Portsmouth Point' cartoon. This image did so much to confirm this area's erstwhile reputation as a sink of drunken excess and debauchery.

> **Retrace your steps to Broad Street.**

Viewed diagonally across the street is a half-timbered building with a

witch's hat turret. This was originally a Brickwoods pub, it later became a restaurant and is now an estate agents office. Perhaps you have there in one building a mini-history of twentieth-century English urban life.

Walking Tour 1

> *Turn left and go back up Broad Street. (To the right is Portsmouth Point an area included in Walking Tour 2). Broad Street curves left into the High Street and brings you out by the Cathedral Church of St Thomas of Canterbury.*

The Cathedral building is almost alone among cathedrals in having a twentieth-century extension. Work on a 1927 design for an extension of the nave was halted by the war. Various post-war designs were considered including one by the designer of Rome's Olympic Stadium, Pier-Luigi Nervi. The more contextual, present extension was completed in 1991. The interior is light and sympathetic and inspired Pevsner, in his *Buildings of Hampshire*, to include some ten pages of description. There is a particularly fine organ and organ loft.

> *Coming out of the cathedral, turn left up the High Street.*

As you walk up the High Street note the existing businesses. In 1896 enterprises on the High Street included Moncks' Oyster Depot, a military cap maker, two booksellers, a sadler, a telegraph office, a haberdasher, a piano-forte teacher, tailors to the Army and Navy, a bookbinder, watch-makers and a shipping insurance agent who doubled as the vice-consul for Germany and Austro-Hungary!

You will soon pass on your left the John Pounds Memorial Unitarian church, with a monument to this pioneering educationalist in the adjoining garden. Cross the road and come to John Mason's house where the Duke of Buckingham was murdered in 1628 by John Felton who was hanged at Tyburn for his crime. A plaque on the greystone façade tells you the story.

> *Continue up the street past the former Cambridge Barracks, now Portsmouth Grammar School's main building. At the Cambridge Junction roundabout turn right into Museum Road.*

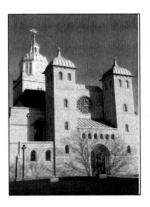

The Cathedral Church of St Thomas, founded in the 1180s, received a modern extension which was completed in 1991.

Walking Tour 1

You will see here the survivor of what was once an extensive city block of an Army township. This North Block of the former Clarence Barracks now houses the City Museum, Art Gallery and Records Office. If you have time the museum is certainly worth a visit. The permanent exhibition tells the story of Portsmouth and the displays include some evocative interiors. There are exhibits on all aspects of local history and there is a gallery devoted to maritime art. Entrance is free and there is a coffee shop and a bookshop.

> *Out of the museum turn left and head back towards Cambridge Junction and cross the road toward the two-storey grey building opposite.*

This building was formerly the wartime NAAFI and is now converted as the University's Students' Union building.

> *At the roundabout turn right into Cambridge Road.*

You will soon come to the University's Frewen Library, seen through the railings on your right. Designed by Ahrends, Burton and Koralek in 1977, it was originally intended to be part of a much larger scheme that would have created a unified campus for the pre-University, Polytechnic, filling all of this city block. The library's interesting ziggurat configuration is best seen from the side, away from the road.

> *Continue further on past the library.*

On your left is Portsmouth's very own dome – this one is an indoor tennis facility. As you approach road the next junction a building site on the right heralds the arrival of a new Students' Union building.

> *At the pedestrian crossing, cross over and skirt around Mercantile House, a 1960s tower on your right, to cross at a further pelican crossing.*

You are now standing in front of Charter House, one of the few remaining large-scale nineteenth-century commercial buildings in Portsmouth. Pevsner describes this as 'exuberantly neo-Flemish'.

Walk past Charter House and cross the dual carriageway at the

pedestrian lights over to A.E. Cogswell's Palace Cinema – now the Uropa Club.

Walking Tour 1

Walk up Guildhall Walk towards Guildhall Square.

On your left you will pass the Theatre Royal, remodelled by Frank Matcham in 1900 and still managing to survive as a working theatre. If there is an opportunity, go inside to see the auditorium – arguably the finest room in Portsmouth. Its next door neighbour, the Prudential Assurance Building (built in 1891), had a Gothic red terracotta and brick façade devised as a company trademark design by Alfred Waterhouse (1830-1905) who was also the architect of the Natural History Museum in London and the town hall in Manchester.

Continue into the Guildhall Square where you might consider a visit to the Guildhall itself to see Berry Webber's remodelled fifties interior. The original interior was destroyed by fire in a bombing raid in 1941. You can visit the foyer, with its Traventine marble walls and Anthony Baynes murals, just by visiting the box office. Ask here for the guided tour which takes you to the auditorium, Council Chamber, Star Chamber with its glass mural depicting the City's history, and the first floor reception room that recalls the opulent transatlantic liner interiors of the Blue Riband era.

Walk down King Henry I Street to the left of the Guildhall to view the University's Park Building.

This was the first purpose built college building in Portsmouth, built originally as the Municipal College in 1908. Standing on the steps of the main entrance you will notice carved into the porch's Portland stone, carved figures representing Mechanics, Drawing, Knowledge, Painting and Chemistry. Go through the main entrance to have a look at the entrance hall with its glazed tile dados. See also the mosaic designs in the floor depicting HMS *Victory* and a Dreadnought battleship.

Retrace your steps along King Henry I Street back to the Guildhall Square, pausing to look back and up at the college entrance tower with its cupola topped by a galleon finial.

WALKING TOUR 2
Seafront Walk: Portsmouth Point to the Hayling Ferry

The walk is about 4 miles long and is mostly along the seafront esplanade. There is a return bus service (No. 15) available if required, but note that the last bus leaves at 15.30 each day.

> **Start in front of the Spice Island pub on Portsmouth Point and begin by walking past the Still and West pub, toward Bath Square.**

The old customs and excise office was near this point and this department would have had a busy time along this coast in days gone by. Early emigrants to North America departed from the nearby quay. The Still and West's name derives, apparently, from a marriage alliance between the landlord of the Still Tavern and the daughter of the landlord of the nearby East and West Country House. The tavern's original name is probably linked to the custom of assembling an honour guard on the upper deck of naval ships entering and leaving the harbour; these sailors were brought to attention by the bosun's whistle or 'still'. There have been many such comings and goings at this place.

Just past the pub on the right was HM Waterguard Office where a customs house has stood since the eighteenth century. On your left is the Portsmouth Sailing Club, formerly the Dutch Consulate building. As you enter Bath Square, you will see the two-storey weather-boarded, Quebec House on the shoreline. Built in 1754, this was a bath house with four sea-bathing rooms that filled with the tide – this was the start of the 'seawater-is-good-for-you' craze. The house was re-named to commemorate the landing at the Point of the body of General Wolfe, the victor of the Battle of Quebec in 1759.

> **Continue along West Street into Tower Street and so past Tower House.**

Tower House is the former home and studio of marine artist William Wyllie. Further along on the right, at the foot of the Round Tower, is Capstan Square. It was here that a capstan was used to raise or lower the protective chain or boom that spanned the harbour mouth, across to Fort Blockhouse on the Gosport side.

*The Sally Port, Old
Portsmouth – a
watergate cut in one of
the eighteen-gun battery
walls.*

**To reach the Round Tower follow the street left to join
the High Street. Turn right and right again and head for
the steps up the wall of the eighteen-gun battery.**

The Round Tower was built in around 1418 and provides the perfect
viewing platform for seeing vessels approaching and leaving the harbour.

**Descend to and walk along the 18-gun, or Sally Port,
Battery towards the Square Tower.**

On the landward side is the usual mix of domestic architectural styles,
including some modern Georgian but Nos 10 and 12 High Street are
worth noticing for their authentic, locally specific and shallow bow
windows; there are two other fine examples on the other side of the
Square Tower. These fortifications were designed originally by Sir Bernard
de Gomme, a Dutch military engineer, in the 1680s and remodelled in
1848-50. With its towers and walkways, this area provides a townscape as
coherent and well-defined as anything in the city.

As you near the Square Tower see, near its base, a chain link sculpture.
This is the Australian Settlers' Memorial and commemorates the sailing
of the First Fleet settlers from Spithead, on 13 May 1787, bound for
Botany Bay. This shipment of 750 convicts was the start of a penal
experiment designed to export England's criminal class – a project that
saw an estimated 160,000 people sent to Australia and Van Diemen's
Land (Tasmania) between 1787 and 1868. Transportable crimes then
included receiving stolen goods, forgery, poaching and minor theft. The

Walking Tour 2

Battery Row terrace, just by the Square Tower, Old Portsmouth.

Statue of Horatio Nelson in Pembroke Gardens, Southsea, looking out towards Long Curtain Battery – his point of embarkation on 14 September 1805.

making of this Georgian and Victorian gulag is brilliantly told by Robert Hughes in *The Fatal Shore*.

Next to the sculpture is the Sallyport, a fortified opening from which to make a 'sally' or sortie. This gave access to the shore from the former walled city and was one of the main embarkation points for ships anchored in Spithead. During the age of sail, negotiating and berthing in the harbour was a difficult operation.

The Square Tower started life in the 1490s as an artillery powder magazine. By 1779 it was being used as a Navy meat store. In 1823 a semaphore station was built on the top to complete a chain of signals between the Admiralty in London and ships at Spithead.

> **Walk around the square tower on the fortified walkway and head east towards the funfair.**

A moat separates you from Long Curtain Battery that was also part of the de Gomme's work in the seventeenth century. It was from here that Nelson set out to join his flagship HMS *Victory* and sail toward his fateful encounter at the Battle of Trafalgar.

> **Head along the promenade to the amusement park now perched on the landing stage.**

Here was once the elegant Clarence Pier, almost completely destroyed by bombing during the Second World War. The original structure was a popular venue with visitors in the late nineteenth and early twentieth

Billy Mannings' funfair.

Walking Tour 2

centuries. It housed assembly rooms, a hotel and steamer landing stage. It is now the site for Billy Mannings' funfair.

As you emerge into the bus terminus at the end of Pier Road, you pass buildings, such as the Jurassic 3001 and signs of a 1950s update of Victorian pier architecture. As you continue south-east along Clarence Parade, you pass the hovercraft terminal. A regular service to the Isle of Wight has operated from here since 1965.

Continue along the parade.

Portsmouth is full of monuments, many commemorating long-forgotten Imperial adventures. As redevelopment and road widening projects have

An Isle of Wight Hovercraft on the slipway on Clarence Esplanade.

Walking Tour 2

Statue of Bernard Law Montgomery of Alamein (1887-1976) near the D-Day Museum.

taken place, some of these have been rounded up into a sort of obelisk corral on the west side of Victoria Park; others dot the seafront. So here, in sequence moving east are some of the ones you will see: the Shannon memorial, to the fallen of Shannon's Naval Brigade during the Indian Mutiny in 1857-8; the Trafalgar memorial, a replica anchor from HMS *Victory*; HMS *Chesapeake* memorial – a stone tribute to the casualties from this ship which saw action in China, Arabia and India between 1857 and 1861; the *Trident* obelisk commemorating the men of HMS *Trident* who died of yellow fever in Sierra Leone in 1859; HMS *Aboukir*'s memorial to the members of the ship's company who died of yellow fever in Jamaica during 1873-74.

Across on the Common is the impressive Royal Navy Memorial, designed by Sir Robert Lorimer, 1920-24, bearing witness to the naval dead of the First World War. The wall that stretches around between two pavilions on the monument's landward side commemorates those who died at sea in the Second World War. There's a poignancy about these stone servicemen with their binoculars and duffle coats. It feels like a significant place.

> **Continue further eastwards, towards the Sealife Centre.**

Here is another memorial, this time for the casualties of the Crimean War (1854-56). This war saw Britain, France, Sardinia and Turkey taking on the Russians over their expansionist ambitions. The siege of Sebastopol, the battle of Balaclava, the Charge of the Light Brigade and other miseries of this war were recorded in the images of photographer Roger Fenton and in the reports of William Russell, the first war correspondent.

The Royal Navy Memorial, Southsea Common.

The money for this memorial was raised by the Portsmouth Debating Society. Ascend the steps on the right of the Tourist Information Centre (open during summer months).

From the top of West Battery, inland, can be viewed a composite landscape of seaside holiday leisure activities; tennis courts, bowling green and putting course. Walking east along the top of the battery you skirt a grass bowl with a bandstand in its centre.

> **Leave the Battery walkway by a ramp that leads to the back of the D-Day Museum (built by Portsmouth City Architects, 1984) and walk round to the front of this building.**

Portsmouth had been the main embarkation point for troops going to the Crimea in 1854 and ninety years later it was a key location for the planning and launch of the invasion of Normandy in June 1944 – D-Day. This offensive is recalled in the D-Day Museum. Entry is by the Sherman tank and over a low bridge. The museum is small-scale, almost domestic in comparison with, say, the Memorial Museum in Caen. There's as much emphasis on Home Front life in the Anderson shelter and wartime memorabilia as there is on the mechanics of the invasion. It's worth visiting the museum for its central exhibit alone - the Overlord Embroidery, a magnificent modern take on the Bayeux Tapestry idea. The work is 272ft long and it took twenty embroiderers five years to make. Food and drink is dispensed from a mock-up NAAFI trailer and there is small shop. (The museum is open daily, except 24-26 December.)

Outside the museum, cross the road to see the small D-Day memorial garden and nearby, on the Avenue de Caen, a statue of the key British player in Operation Overlord, Field Marshal Bernard Montgomery, and Garrison Commander in Portsmouth, just prior to the outbreak of war. *(This may be a convenient place on the walk to take a refreshment break. Walk up this road and cross into Palmerston Road where restaurants, sandwich shops, bakeries and pubs proliferate).*

> **Back at the D-Day Museum, head eastwards again toward Southsea Castle, passing the ornamental lake.**

Southsea Castle was built in 1544, the Portsmouth link in a chain of coastal defence forts assembled by Henry VIII. Until 1830 when the area was drained and levelled, the castle was surrounded by salt marsh and heathland. In 1884 the Corporation leased the castle from the

Walking Tour 2

government. The open aspect of the surrounding land was preserved through a War Department edict which forbade any building on seafront land that could mask the effectiveness of the guns of the castle and other forts. A lighthouse to house a fixed, permanent light was constructed here in the !920s. The lighthouse keeper and his family lived in two rooms just inside the castle's gate. The castle was restored by the City's Architects' Department between 1960 and 1967 and now operates as a museum. Look out for announcements of Civil War re-enactment displays that often take place here in the summer.

> **From the castle follow the path up onto the crest of the eastern rampart.**

From here you will be rewarded with a 360-degree panorama: west to Old Portsmouth, across to the Clarence Parade edge of built-up Southsea, Castle field where Zeppelin spotters once looked out, the beach to South Parade Pier and out over the Spithead and the Solent.

> **Walk along the rampart and down onto the Esplanade that leads towards the Pier.**

You reach this by passing some contrasting examples of seaside visitor attractions from different eras! The Pyramids Centre, a modern water sports facility, is neighbour to rock gardens and a trio of seafront, cast iron and timber shelters, built for the use of visitors in around 1900. South Parade Pier has seen better days, but is a local survivor of that uniquely British invention, the seaside pier. The original pier was designed by George Rake and opened in 1879. A fire in 1904 meant complete replacement and a second elegant Edwardian pier, designed by G.E. Smith and billed as a 'summer pleasure pier' and a 'winter palace', was opened four years later. Fire dashed the pier's fortunes after the Second World War.

> **Walk eastwards along the Esplanade and cross by the bus terminus to see the rather modest D-Day gardens and stone, unveiled in 1948. Cross to the Canoe Lake past the Emanuel Fountain.**

This is a memorial to the first Jewish mayor of Portsmouth who, during his time on the council from 1841 until the end of 1860s, was a prime

mover behind the construction of the Esplanade, the levelling of Southsea Common and the creation of the People's Park (now renamed Victoria Park). His career marked the beginning of a long and almost continuous period of Jewish involvement in Portsmouth's civic affairs. The Canoe Lake with its hire boats, swans, teas and ice-creams, children's play area and model village beyond, provides the familiar facilities of the seaside holiday. Skirting the lake walk behind the café and through the garden that takes you past the distinctive-looking butterfly house, to the Natural History Museum. The museum has a small display ranging from a model *Iguanodon* to the 'urban desert'.

> **From the museum walk further eastwards along Eastern parade.**

On your right a summer sports landscape unfolds – a bowling green, lawn tennis courts and a cricket ground. On the left, in turn, are Bruce, Spencer and Helena Roads and Cousins and Burbidge Groves containing substantial bourgeois villas. Look out for one – opposite the path between the tennis and the cricket ground – reminiscent of the Spanish Colonial Revival houses of Los Angeles! Beyond the cricket ground, and by Southsea's minigolf links, is the perfect place to have lunch or tea at the aptly-named Tenth Hole Tea Room (open seven days a week, 9 a.m. to 4.30 p.m. (closed January).

> **Walk eastwards along Eastern Parade and opposite the apex of the mini-golf course cross to Eastney Esplanade. Cross at the pedestrian crossing and walk east along the Esplanade.**

Now on the left appears the magnificence of the former Royal Marines Barracks, Eastney. The first substantial terrace with the mock-machiolated water tower behind, was the officers' staff quarter. Further east a long, soldiers' dormitory block faces the parade ground. This has now been redeveloped as housing by Redrow who, with advice from English Heritage, have succeeded in retaining the coherence of the design of this military township. Alan Balfour described it as a 'forceful urban environment' and it compares well with anything in Portsmouth's civilian cityscape.

In 1664 Charles II approved the formation of the Duke of York and Albany's Maritime Regiment of Foot (the Royal Marines). Subsequently these sea soldiers have participated in diverse and significant military engagements and voyages of the last three centuries, including Captain Cook's expeditions, guarding the convicts of the First Fleet, the Crimean

Walking Tour 2

War, the Boer War, Gallipoli and the Zeebrugge raid in the First World War. They were also prominent in special forces raids in the Second World War, D-Day and the recapture of the Falklands.

Their final departure from these barracks was in October 1991. In its heyday, this 1½ mile long site was a self-contained military enclave. The officers' mess is suitably grand with the central section faced in Portland stone and has an imposing stone stair entrance to the *piano nobile*. This grandeur was continued inside with a full-height central stair hall with two flights of stairs leading to an upper dining room and orchestra platform. All this can now be seen because the mess is home to the Royal Marines Museum. The entrance is signalled by a statue of the 'Yomper'.

Go in and have a look; there are medal displays, tableaux, interactive displays, artefacts, weapons. The building's interior itself is really the star exhibit, its lavish decoration and design redolent of the lifestyle led by officers of a privileged time. The mess once hosted the last German Kaiser, Wilhelm II who, in 1890, watched from here a war game unfolding on the adjoining drill field. If you are seeking refreshment the lawn makes a good picnic site and there's licensed restaurant – The Bugle Major. The museum is open every day (except 25, 26 December) 10 a.m. – 5 p.m. (4.30 p.m. Sept-May).

> *Leaving Eastney Barracks, turn left and continue eastwards along the Esplanade. The now road curves inland, passing Eastney swimming baths on your right. Turn right into Neville Road and continue past the caravan park to join Fort Cumberland Road. Keep walking in the direction of the ferry, with the shrubland of a disused rifle and gunnery range on your right. Soon you will come to Langstone Marina on your left and opposite, the unassuming entrance to Fort Cumberland.*

The fort keeps such a low profile in the landscape that it is inconspicuous from the main road. The fort was built under the direction of the Duke of Cumberland in 1746 to defend the entrance to Langstone harbour. Although the fort includes an English Heritage Archaeology Centre, it is not normally open to the public. The fort opens occasionally for pre-booked guided tours only (Tel. 01483-252015).

It is worth making an effort to get access because, even in its unreconstructed state, this fort is a stunning piece of military geometry and gives unrivalled views over Hayling Bay, Langstone Harbour, Portsdown Hill and the Solent. This twenty-four acre, star-shaped fort (a 'wide pentagon') is arguably one of the finest pieces of surviving defensive architecture in the country, it demands a new role.

From the fort continue walking towards the Hayling Island ferry. You will soon come to the lifeboat station and after that some houseboats and the ferry landing stage itself.

Looking around you will see a tower block across Eastney Lake; this student hall of residence signals the University's Langstone Campus. Looking out over Langstone Harbour you will see a concrete 'caisson' randomly deposited just north of the ferry route. This was made as one of the many pre-constructed sections for the Mulberry Harbour docking facilities, built for the D-Day landings but for some reason this one didn't make it to France.

Langstone Harbour is a natural neighbour and complement to Portsmouth's urbanism. Its shoreline of mudland and saltmarshes provides an important wildlife habitat. At the top of the harbour, Farlington Marshes is a way station for migrating birds and there is a profusion of types – Brent geese, shelducks, goldeneyes, little terns, oyster catchers, redshanks – which in turn draws flocks of bird watchers to see them.

On the Langstone shores there were valuable and productive salterns, or salt-works, and oyster beds too were harvested. Smuggling sometimes provided an alternative earner although the sentries of Fort Cumberland and the coastguard cutter patrols did their best to control it!

There are strong currents between Ferry Point and Eastney beach and there have been schemes to provide both bridges and a vehicle conveyer system, none of which materialised. There is presently a motor-boat service for cyclists and walking passengers between the islands which is an efficient and environmentally friendly option.

Here the walk ends and to return to your starting point you will need to catch a no. 15 bus from near the lifeboat station.

The Next Steps

Places to Visit

The Dockyard contains:

The Royal Naval Museum, HMS *Victory*, HMS *Warrior*, the *Mary Rose*, Ship Hall and Museum (Tel. Flagship Portsmouth 023 9286 1512 or www.flagship.org.uk)

Portsmouth City Museum, Museum Road, Portsmouth (Tel. 023 9282 7261)

Treadgolds & Co, Bishop Street, Portsmouth. Victorian ironmonger's business preserved as a museum (Tel. 023 9282 4745)

Charles Dickens Birthplace Museum, Old Commercial Road, Portsmouth (Tel. 023 9282 7261)

D-Day Museum and Overlord Embroidery (Tel. 023 9282 7261)

Southsea Castle (Tel. 023 9282 7261)

Portchester Castle (English Heritage – Tel. 023 9237 8291)

Fort Nelson, Down End Road, Fareham – at Palmerston Fort, Royal Armouries Museum of Artillery (Tel. 01329 233734)

Fort Brockhurst, Gosport – a Palmerston Fort (English Heritage – Tel. 023 9258 1059)

The Royal Marines Museum and Eastney Barracks (Tel. 023 9281 9385)

Royal Navy Submarine Museum, Gosport (Tel. 023 9252 9217, www.rnsubmus.co.uk)

Eastney Beam Engine House – open last complete weekend of every month (Tel. 023 9282 7261)

Research

Portsmouth City Museum and Record Office, Museum Road, Portsmouth (Tel. 023 9282 7261)

General Portsmouth museums information (Tel. 023 9282 7261 or www.portsmouthmuseums.co.uk)

Hampshire Record Office, Sussex Street, Winchester, and West Sussex Record Office, Orchard Street, Chichester, hold archive records for Portsmouth and Gosport (HRO Tel. 01962 846154/WSRO Tel. 01243 753600)

Admiralty Library, Portsmouth Naval Base, Portsmouth (Tel. 023 9272 7577)

Portsmouth Oral History Network (Contact: Sharon Lee, Oral History Co-ordinator, tel. 023 9282 7261)

Bibliography

Essential reading are the *Portsmouth Papers*, a treasure trove of Portsmouth local history: from Paper 1, *Portchester Castle* by Barry Cunliffe (1967), through Paper 68, *W.L. Wyllie: The Portsmouth Years* by Nigel Grundy (1996) to Paper 70, *Railways and Portsmouth Society 1847-1947* by R.C. Riley (2000). They are published by Portsmouth City Council and available from libraries and museum shops.

Spithead: an Informal History by Michael Lewis (George Allen and Unwin, 1972) is just this.

Fisher's Face by Jan Morris (Viking, 1995) is a short, highly readable account of the life of 'Jacky' Fisher – mostly biography, in part a love letter

Crossing the Harbour by Lesley Burton and Brian Musselwhite is a history of the Harbour from a Gosport perspective

A.E. Cogswell: Architect Within a Victorian City by Andy Nash (Portsmouth Polytechnic School of Architecture, 1975)

In a Free State: The Architecture and Life of G.E. Smith by Anthony Clelford (Portsmouth Polytechnic School of Architecture, 1982)

Portsmouth in the Twentieth Century: a Photographic History by John Stedman (Halsgrove, 1999) has an excellent text to accompany over 300 photographs. Among several old photograph histories of Portsmouth this one stands out

George Marston: Shackleton's Antarctic Artist by Stephen Locke (Hampshire County Council: Hampshire Papers No. 19, 2000)

Publications about the **Second World War and Portsmouth** are numerous but recommended are:

City at War by Nigel Peake (Milestone Publications, 1986)

Battle over Portsmouth: a City at War in 1940 (Middleton Press, 1986)

The Battle of the Atlantic: The Corvettes and their Crews: An Oral History by Chris Howard-Bailey for the Royal Naval Museum (Sutton Publishing, 1994)

Operation Overlord: The History of D-Day and the Overlord Embroidery by Stephen Brooks and Eve Eckstein (Ashford, 1989)

For the history of **Southsea**:

The Growth of Southsea as a Naval Satellite and Victorian Resort by Ray Riley (*Portsmouth Papers* 16, 1972)

The Houses and Inhabitants of Thomas Ellis Owen's Southsea by Ray Riley (*Portsmouth Papers* 32, 1980)

Southsea Past by Sarah Quail (Phillimore, 2000) integrates fine illustrations with a primary source-based text

The Invisible Woman: The Story of Nelly Ternan and Charles Dickens by Claire Tomalin (Penguin Books, 1990) is a fascinating work of historical detection

People's Palaces: The Story of the Seaside Pleasure Buildings of 1870-1914 by Lynn F. Pearson (Barracuda Books, 1991)

Amusement Machines by Lynn F. Pearson (Shire Publications, 1992)

The Origins of Portsmouth and the First Charter by Sarah Quail (City of Portsmouth, 1994) details the lives of Jean de Gisors and Richard I as they affected the development of Portsmouth.

'Palmerston's Folly': The Portsdown and Spithead Forts by Professor A. Temple Patterson (*Portsmouth Papers* 3, 1980) for a brilliant telling of the forts saga – it should perhaps be compulsory reading for all politicians and voters!

The Heyday of Steam: Victoria's Navy by Colin White (Kenneth Mason, 1983) is worth seeking out

The Royal Navy: An Illustrated Social History 1870-1982 by Capt. John Wells (Alan Sutton, 1994) is useful

Treadgolds: The Development and Decline of a Portsea Ironmongers 1800-1988 by Ann Day (*Portsmouth Papers* 67, 1995) is a fascinating study

The Anglican Revival in Victorian Portsmouth by Nigel Yates (*Portsmouth Papers* 37, 1983) is a fascinating account of zealous evangelicals, devout Anglo-Catholics and pioneering urban missionaries

Votes for Women: The Women's Fight in Portsmouth by Sarah Peacock (*Portsmouth Papers* 39, 1983) charts the struggle to get the women's suffrage issue onto the political agenda

Useful for an understanding of **Portsmouth's history and its natural context** are:

The Portsmouth Region by Barry Stapleton and James H. Thomas (eds) (Alan Sutton, 1989), a reader covering archaeology, history, geology and ecology

The Spirit of Portsmouth: a History by J. Webb *et al.* (Phillimore, 1989) is a themed approach to the city's history

Railways and Portsmouth Society 1847-1947 by Ray Riley (*Portsmouth Papers* 70, 2000) is an informative look at the railways' social consequences for Portsmouth

The Wooden World: An Anatomy of the Georgian Navy, by N.A.M. Rodger (Fontana, 1988) is a readable and balanced account

Nelson's Navy: The Ships, Men and Organisation 1793-1815 by Brian Lavery (Conway Maritime, 1989) is encyclopaedic on the subject

Books on **Nelson and the Georgian Navy** are numerous but the following are noteworthy:

Nelson: The Immortal Memory By David and Stephen Howarth (Conway Maritime, 1988) is a good straightforward account

The Nelson Companion edited by Colin White (Alan Sutton, 1995) includes essays on the legend, relics, memorabilia, monuments and biographical sites

Duisburg: So wie es war by Gertrud Milkereit (Droste Verlag, 1986) tells and shows it as it was

Oral history research is strong in Portsmouth: Dockyard memories collected by Ann Day, Ken Lunn and their students at the University have been published as:

Inside the Wall: Recollections of Portsmouth Dockyard 1900-1950 (History Research Centre, University of Portsmouth, 1998)

Staying Afloat: Recollections of Portsmouth Dockyard 1950-Present (HRC, University of Portsmouth, 1999)

The Evolution of the Docks and Industrial Buildings in Portsmouth Royal Dockyard 1698-1914 (*Portsmouth Papers* 44, 1985) by Ray Riley is very useful

Portsmouth Reborn: Destruction and Reconstruction: 1939-1974 by John Stedman (*Portsmouth Papers* 66, 1995) is a good account of the destruction and rebuilding

Finally, now out of print but worth looking out for, is:

Portsmouth by Alan Balfour (Studio Vista, 1970), a sensitive cataloguing of key sites in the city before 'Heritage' was the watchword.

Index